the **OXO**
book of
food
& cooking

**first published in
Great Britain by**

Simon & Schuster, 1996
A Viacom Company
Copyright © Van den Bergh
Foods Ltd

Simon & Schuster Ltd
West Garden Place
Kendal Street
London W2 2AQ

ISBN 0 85941 921 5

Text: Lorna Rhodes
Design: Green Moore Lowenhoff
Illustrations: Peter Byatt
Photography: Karl Adamson
Typesetting: Stylize
Styling: Maria Kelly
Food preparation: Lorna Rhodes
Printed and bound in the UK by
Bath Press Colourbooks

recipe notes

All the recipes in this cookbook give ingredients in both metric and imperial measures. Use either one set of measurements or the other, but not a mixture of both in any one recipe.

All teaspoons and tablespoons are level, unless otherwise stated. 1 teaspoon = 5 ml; 1 tablespoon = 15 ml.

Egg size is medium unless otherwise stated. Vegetables and fruit are medium-size unless otherwise stated.

The preparation and cooking times are included as a general guide, but preparation times especially are approximate. The calories per serving are also approximate and are calculated based on a medium-size serving.

contents

contents

chapter 3 fish

chapter 4 vegetables

contents

chapter 5 rice & pasta

chapter 6 eggs & cheese

Oxo to the rescue!

Any good home cook will tell you that for really tasty, wholesome home-made stews, casseroles, hot-pots, pies and bakes, you have to start with a good flavoursome stock. All the rich and savoury taste of the stock will end up in your cooking – it's hard to go wrong. (If you're not sure about this, try making a home-made soup with Oxo stock and then try making it with water – one is full of flavour, it's warming and hearty: the other is frankly, well, watery.)

Good stock is something Oxo know a thing or two about – they've been making stock cubes for long enough; 85 years to be exact. So if you want a guarantee of empty plates at the end of every suppertime, you want to start with a rich Oxo stock.

And inside Oxo's new *Book of Food and Cooking* you'll find plenty of recipes that do just that – recipes for dishes such as Lamb Casserole with Leek Scones, Sausage and Mushroom Crumble and American Chicken Pie. You'll also find some exciting new ideas, like a balti-inspired Quick Chicken Curry you can put together in a jiffy and a great recipe from the States, Herby Mince Popovers (like baby Yorkshire puds with a tasty meatball in the middle).

And, because Oxo know just how hard it is at the end of a busy day to find the time or energy to cook, there are plenty of tips, and advice on freezing and microwaving to help you cut down on the hours spent in the kitchen.

But *The Oxo Book of Food and Cooking* is much more than a collection of recipes. If you've ever thumbed through a cookbook wondering why they never explain the basics, such as poaching an egg, then look no further. At the beginning of each chapter we've included an 'All you need to know' section containing, quite simply, all you need to know on buying, storing, preparing and cooking meat, poultry, fish, vegetables, rice and pasta, and eggs and cheese. There's information on nutrition too; and clear step-by-step photographs whenever there's a tricky bit.

So whenever you're racking your brains for ideas of things to cook – but can't seem to get beyond beans on toast; or whenever you discover that your cooking skills seem to be a bit lacking in one department or another; whenever in fact you're plagued by that inescapable question 'What shall I cook today?', don't despair. Have a quick flick through *The Oxo Book of Food and Cooking*. You've got the question – we've got fifty-six brilliant answers!

meat
all you need to know:
choosing & storing meat

meat and a healthy diet

Meat's main contribution to our diet is that of protein. Meat also contains vitamins B6 and B12, iron and zinc. In recent years, meat has been regarded as high in fat, particularly saturated fat. In fact, however, the levels of saturated fat in meat vary a great deal, according to both the cut of meat and cooking method. If you pay attention to the total amount of saturated fat in your diet, there is no reason why you cannot enjoy meat regularly.

buying meat

Always buy meat from a reputable butcher or supermarket to ensure that you are getting good-quality meat that has been kept in refrigerated and hygienic conditions. Using a butcher has the advantage of giving you access to hands-on advice about cuts of meat etc. However, supermarkets often provide leaflets with information and recipes to go along with their pre-packed cuts, and many now have fresh-meat counters to give a wider choice. When buying pre-packed meat, always check the 'use-by' date.

When buying meat off the bone, allow 100-225 g (4-8 oz per person).

choosing meat

Meat should look and smell fresh – avoid any that appears dry or has a grey tinge. However, a bright-red colour does not necessarily indicate good

quality. Beef, for example, gets darker when it is hung, which is very important in developing flavour and improving texture.

It goes almost without saying that you need to consider the type of recipe you have in mind when choosing a cut of meat. There are several considerations. How much time do you have? Tender cuts of meat (e.g., veal, new-season lamb or rump steak) are suitable for quick cooking methods such as grilling or frying. Are you trying to cut down on fat? These young cuts tend to be lean and have a fine

grain. What about cost? Unfortunately, these same cuts are likely to be the most expensive. Cheaper cuts are often those tougher or older ones that require a longer, slower cooking. Cuts such as chuck steak or oxtail can't be hurried, but, when properly cooked, they will take on a far more complicated, richer flavour than the quick-cooking tender cuts.

Minced meat can be made from beef, veal, pork and lamb. The colour of minced beef is a good indication of its quality – the paler it is the higher its fat content. Most supermarkets label minced beef according to its fat content, which is usually between 5 and 20 per cent. Lean mince is the best for use in most recipes; it's both healthier, and you avoid having an oily surface on dishes such as bolognaise sauce.

storing meat

Once bought, put frozen meat in the freezer, or fresh meat in the refrigerator, as soon as possible. Place fresh meat from the butcher in a shallow container and wrap it loosely in plastic film. Take care that meat juices do not drip on to any other food. Sealed packs should be left unopened and consumed by the 'use-by' date on the label. Meat should be kept in the coldest part of your refrigerator, and the temperature should not rise above 5°C/41°F.

Raw minced meat and offal are especially perishable and should be used within one day of purchase

Beef, lamb, pork and sausages can be kept for three days and bacon for up to one week.

Frozen meat can be stored for up to nine months in the freezer; check the 'use-by' date on ready-frozen meat.

Food that is warm or at room temperature provides an ideal breeding-ground for bacteria. Cool any cooked meat for later eating as quickly as possible and then refrigerate it. Use it within two days and re-heat it thoroughly before eating.

all you need to know:
preparing & cooking meat

roasting

It is essential to choose a good-quality, tender cut of meat for roasting. Allow about 225 g (8 oz) per person for a boned and rolled joint, or 300–350 g (10–12 oz) per person for meat on the bone. If you are hesitant about carving, choose a boned and rolled joint which will be easy to slice.

Traditionally, string was used to hold together boned and rolled joints. In most cases this has been replaced by an elastic netting. The Meat and Livestock Commission recommends leaving the netting in place while the meat is cooking but removing it before carving.

For best results, use the following cuts for roasting:
Beef: sirloin, fore (best) or wing (prime) ribs, topside, fillet
Lamb: leg, loin, saddle, best end, shoulder, breast
Pork: loin, fillet, spare ribs, shoulder, neck end

easy steps to a perfect roast
● Bring the meat to room temperature before cooking.
● Preheat the oven to 220°C/425°F/Gas Mark 7.
● Weigh the joint, including any stuffing, and calculate the cooking time (see the table below).
● Season the meat and apply aromatic flavourings, e.g., rubbing beef with mustard, studding lamb with slivers of garlic and rosemary sprigs (see picture below); and rubbing pork with salt and oil.

● Place the meat, fat-side up on a rack in a roasting tin, and brush it lightly with oil or melted fat.
● Cook the meat for 15 minutes, to sear the outside.
● Lower the oven temperature to 180°C/350°F/Gas Mark 4 and continue to cook.
● Baste the meat with the cooking juices several times during roasting (see picture below).

● When the joint is cooked, transfer it to a board, carving dish or warm serving plate. Cover it with foil to keep it warm and allow to stand for 10–15 minutes, while you make the gravy.

Roasting chart

Beef		
	Rare	20 minutes per 450 g/1 lb + 20 minutes
	Medium	25 minutes per 450 g/1 lb + 25 minutes
	Well done	30 minutes per 450 g/1 lb + 30 minutes
Lamb	Medium	25 minutes per 450 g/1 lb + 25 minutes
	Well done	30 minutes per 450 g/1 lb + 30 minutes
Pork	Medium	30 minutes per 450 g/1 lb + 30 minutes
	Well done	35 minutes per 450 g/1 lb + 35 minutes

making gravy

● Drain off most of the fat from the pan, leaving about 2 tablespoons of the roasting juices (see picture below).

● Make up 300 ml (½ pint) of Oxo stock by crumbling 2 Oxo cubes into a measuring jug and adding boiling water. Add the stock to the juices and bring to the boil. Stir vigorously to loosen any caramelised cooking juices from the bottom of the roasting tin (see picture below).

● Blend a little cornflour with one tablespoon of water and add it to the gravy, stirring constantly until it thickens. Check the seasoning and serve piping hot.

● For extra flavour, use vegetable cooking liquor to dilute the Oxo cube and add a glass of wine to the stock.

● For a thicker gravy, stir 1–2 tablespoons of plain flour in with the roasting juices and stir vigorously. Cook for one minute and then add the stock gradually, stirring constantly until it reaches the boil. Check the seasoning before serving.

pot-roasting

Pot-roasting is suitable for tougher cuts of meat. Slow cooking over a gentle heat dissolves the tough connective tissues and gives pot-roasts their distinctive thick, rich flavour. Use a flameproof casserole with a tightly fitting lid.

For best results, use the following cuts:
Beef: topside, silverside, brisket
Pork: spare ribs, blade, bacon or gammon joints

easy steps to a perfect pot-roast

● Preheat the oven to 170°C/ 325°F/Gas Mark 3.
● Heat a couple of tablespoons of oil in a flameproof casserole.
● Brown the meat on all sides in the hot oil (see picture below).

Remove it from the pot.
● Reduce the heat and add chopped onions, carrots and celery. Brown them for a few minutes, and stir to scrape any caramelised meat juices from the bottom of the casserole.
● Put the meat back in the casserole.
● Make up 600 ml (1 pint) of Oxo stock and pour it in.
● Add wine, if you like, and any other flavourings such as herbs, garlic cloves, peppercorns etc. Bring back to a gentle boil.
● Cover the casserole tightly and put it in the oven for about 2½ hours, depending on the cut and its size. The meat is cooked when it feels tender when pierced with a fine skewer.

● Transfer the meat to a carving board and keep it warm while you make the gravy.

● Either remove the vegetables to a dish to serve alongside the meat, or push them through a sieve back into the cooking liquid, to thicken and flavour it. Alternatively, blend 2 teaspoons of cornflour with a little water and stir it into the liquid. Simmer on top of the stove until thickened and season, if necessary.

● Carve the meat after about 15 minutes.

braising and casseroling

Casseroles are excellent for family meals because they use cheaper cuts of meat and can be left to cook with little attention. They also reheat well.

Supermarkets often label meat either 'stewing' or 'braising' without specifying the exact cut. Stewing meat requires longer cooking in slightly more liquid, while braising meat is generally leaner. Supermarkets often sell 'boneless, cubed' meat which is ideal for both these kinds of cooking. Ask your butcher for braising or stewing meat, or see below for the names of suitable cuts.

For best results, use the following cuts for braising and stewing:

Beef: neck and clod, shin, chuck, blade, thick or thin flank

Lamb: scrag and middle neck for stewing; shoulder, leg, loin chops and chump chops for braising

Pork: neck end, hand and spring, knuckle end of leg

easy steps to a perfect casserole

● Preheat the oven to 170°C/325°F/Gas Mark 3 if you want to cook the dish in the oven.

● Trim the meat of any sinew, gristle and large lumps of fat (see picture below). Cut

the meat in 2.5 cm (1-inch) cubes, or in slightly larger pieces if you prefer.

● Heat a couple of tablespoons of oil in a large frying pan.

● Brown the meat in the hot oil on all sides (see picture below).

Lift it out with a slotted spoon and transfer it to a casserole. This is an important stage if the casserole is to have good flavour and colour.

● Reduce the heat and add chopped onions, carrots and celery, with extra oil if necessary. Brown the vegetables for a few minutes and then transfer them to the casserole.

● Add a tablespoon of flour to the pan and stir to scrape up any caramelised meat juices (see picture below).

● Make up enough Oxo stock to cover the meat and vegetables, allowing for a little evaporation. If adding pulses to your casserole, bear in mind that they will absorb a lot of stock, and keep an eye on the liquid level throughout cooking. Pour the stock into the pan gradually, as if making a roux-based sauce, and add any additional flavourings.

● Bring to a simmer and pour into the casserole.

● Cover the casserole tightly and cook it in the oven or on top of the stove over a very gentle heat for 2–3 hours.

● Add more delicate vegetables, 15–30 minutes before the end of cooking.

● Check the seasoning and consistency of the casserole. If it is too liquid, reduce it by cooking it uncovered for a while. If it looks too thick, or even a bit dry, gradually add more stock, water or wine, stirring well, until the casserole is reheated and has the consistency you like. Use the same technique for braising, but use larger pieces of meat and less liquid. Braised cuts usually need less cooking.

frying, grilling and barbecuing

Use the most tender cuts of meat for these quick methods of cooking.

Meat that is destined for the grill or barbecue will benefit from being marinated. Marinating or steeping meat in an acidic liquid (e.g. wine, vinegar or fruit juice) helps to tenderise it, and the aromatic flavourings in the marinade (garlic, herbs, spices, etc.) are absorbed by the meat (see picture below).

The longer you marinate, the more tender and flavourful the meat will be. The minimum time for marinating is 1–2 hours at room temperature – overnight in the refrigerator is best. Remember that no amount of marinating will transform an unsuitable cut of meat into a successful barbecued or grilled dish.

easy steps for a perfect fry-up, grill or barbecue

● Remove the meat from the marinade and pat it dry, so that the meat will brown nicely on the outside. Use the marinade for basting or as the basis of a sauce.

● Before grilling, brush with melted butter or oil, season and cook under a preheated, medium-hot grill or on a barbecue, turning at least once. When brown on all sides, you can reduce the heat.

For best results use the following cuts for frying, grilling and barbecuing:
Beef: steaks, including rump, sirloin and fillet
Lamb: cutlets, loin and chump chops, leg steaks, shoulder steaks, neck fillet
Pork: loin chops, fillet (sliced into medallions)

all you need to know:
carving meat

general principles
● For successful carving, you will need a two-pronged fork with a safety guard, and a sharp, long-bladed knife.

● The aim in carving a joint of meat is to cut across the grain, i.e. to cut through the long 'fibres' which are visible in the meat. This makes the meat easier to chew and seem more tender.

● Make sure the meat is secure on a board or plate, and placed on a firm surface so that it won't slip. A spiked meat dish – which anchors the joint firmly – is ideal.

● Remove any string, net or skewers and try to loosen the meat around the bone before carving (see picture below).

● Cut at right angles to the bone if you're able, although this will depend on the shape of the joint (see picture below).

carving boneless joints
This is easy: simply cut across it in slices of whatever thickness you prefer.

carving beef
Fore rib: to carve a small joint, remove the meat from the bone and slice it horizontally. For a large joint, run the knife between the meat and rib bones (see picture below).

Stand the meat, rib-side down, and carve vertical slices between the ribs (see picture below).

Sirloin: if it still has the T-shaped bone, loosen the meat from the bone and carve along the joint (see picture below).

carving legs
The legs of lamb, pork and veal are carved similarly.

● Place the leg fatty-side up and hold the knuckle with one hand.
● Cut a V-shape out of the middle of the top of the

meat (see picture above). Carve slices of meat from both sides of the V (see picture below).

● Turn the leg over and carve the underside in large horizontal slices.

Legs can also be cut in diagonal slices from the knuckle end.

carving loins
These are generally cooked on the bone to prevent shrinkage.

● Cut the meat off the rib cage (see picture below) and slice it. When carving pork, remove the crackling before carving the meat.

carving shoulders
● Place the joint skin-side up. Cut a wedge through the middle of the joint, in the angle between the shoulder blade and the leg bone (see picture below).

● Carve from both sides (see picture below), before turning the joint over to cut horizontal slices from the underside.

lamb casserole with leek scones These leek scones make a delicious accompaniment to the casserole.

2 tablespoons oil
900 g (2 lb) boned leg of lamb, cut in 4 cm (1/2-inch) cubes
2 tablespoons seasoned flour
2 medium-size onions, sliced
225 g (8 oz) mushrooms, sliced thickly
1 Original Oxo cube
1/2 teaspoon dried rosemary
salt and pepper

For the leek scones
40 g (1 1/2 oz) butter
100 g (4 oz) trimmed leeks, chopped finely
100 g (4 oz) self-raising flour
1 teaspoon baking powder
1 Vegetable Oxo cube
1 egg
2 tablespoons milk
oil for frying

❶ Heat the oil in a flameproof casserole. Toss the lamb in the seasoned flour to coat and cook until lightly browned all over. Remove with a slotted spoon and set aside.
❷ Add the onions to the pan and cook gently for about 5 minutes until soft. Add the mushrooms and return the lamb to the pan.

❸ Crumble the Original Oxo cube into 300 ml (1/2 pint) boiling water. Pour the stock into the pan, stir in the rosemary and season. Cover and simmer for 1 hour, or until the meat is tender.
❹ Meanwhile prepare the scones. Melt 15 g (1/2 oz) of the butter in a pan and cook the leeks for 7 minutes until softened. Allow them to cool.
❺ Sift the flour and baking powder into a bowl. Crumble in the Vegetable Oxo cube, add the rest of the butter and rub together until the mixture resembles fine breadcrumbs. Add the cooled leeks. Beat the egg and milk and add it to the mixture to make a soft dough.
❻ Heat a large heavy-based frying pan, brush it with oil and then spoon in the dough in 8 portions. Flatten them slightly with a palette knife. Cook over a low heat for about 4–5 minutes on each side – use the palette knife to turn them over. They are ready when they are golden brown. Serve with the casserole.

Serves 4
Preparation time: 20 minutes + 1 1/4 hours cooking
Calories per serving 640

(OXO) **Tip**
To save preparation time look for ready diced lamb in your supermarket.

Microwave Tip
Seal the lamb and cook the onions in a frying pan. Transfer them to a microwave dish with the remaining ingredients. Cover and cook on MEDIUM (50%) for 30–40 minutes, stirring often, until the meat is tender. Cook scones as directed in recipe.

Freezing Tip
You can prepare the casserole in advance (without the leek scones). Allow it to cool thoroughly before freezing.

leg of lamb with spicy apricot stuffing Ask your butcher to prepare the lamb in advance for you, or you may be able to find boned leg of lamb at your supermarket.

1.5 kg (3¹/₂ lb) leg of lamb, boned

For the stuffing
1 tablespoon sunflower oil
1 small onion, chopped finely
1 garlic clove, crushed, or
1 Oxo Garlic, Herb and Spice cube
1 Oxo Indian Herb and Spice cube
100 g (4 oz) ready-to-eat dried apricots, chopped
40 g (1¹/₂ oz) blanched almonds, chopped
100 g (4 oz) fresh breadcrumbs
2 tablespoons chopped parsley
salt and pepper

❶ Preheat the oven to 200°C/400°F/Gas Mark 6.
❷ Heat the oil in a small saucepan. Add the onion and garlic (if using) and cook for 3 minutes until softened. Otherwise crumble in the Oxo Garlic, Herb and Spice cube with the onion. Crumble in the Oxo Indian Herb and Spice cube and cook for 1 minute more. Turn into a bowl and add the apricots, almonds, breadcrumbs and parsley. Season with salt and pepper.

❸ Lay the meat flat, skin-side down, and spread the stuffing over the top. Roll up the sides to make a neat parcel and tie with string to secure.
❹ Weigh the lamb and calculate the cooking time (page 10). Place the lamb on a rack in a roasting tin and brush the top with oil.
❺ Roast for 15 minutes and then reduce the temperature and continue to cook at 180°C/350°F/Gas Mark 4, basting twice during cooking.
❻ Lift the joint on to a carving board. Cover with foil and allow to stand for 10 minutes. Remove the string before carving (as this is a boneless joint you should have no trouble carving it) and serve with green vegetables.

Serves 4–6
Preparation time: 10 minutes + 2 hours cooking
Calories per serving 525–680

(OXO) **Tip**
You could also use this stuffing in a boned shoulder or crown of lamb.

Microwave Tip
Cook the onion and oil in a dish for 2 minutes on HIGH (100%) until softened. Crumble in the seasoning cubes and cook for 1 minute more. Make the stuffing as directed and then stuff, roll and tie the lamb. Place on a rack in a microwave baking dish and cook on MEDIUM-HIGH (70%) for 20–30 minutes, or until a meat thermometer inserted in the centre reaches 57°C (135°F). For medium-rare meat, cover the lamb in foil and let stand until temperature rises to 65–68°C (150–155°F).

steak and kidney pie In this recipe the meat is cooked slowly to tenderise it before the pastry is added.

3 tablespoons olive oil

700 g (1½ lb) lean chuck
or braising steak, trimmed
of fat and cut in 2.5 cm
(1-inch) cubes

225 g (8 oz) pig's or ox kidney,
cut in small cubes

1 large onion, chopped

25 g (1 oz) flour

2 Original Oxo cubes

1 tablespoon chopped parsley

225 g (8 oz) frozen puff
pastry, thawed

1 small egg, beaten

salt and pepper

❶ Heat the oil in a frying pan and brown the steak and kidney a few pieces at a time until they are browned all over. Lift the pieces out when done and set aside.

❷ Fry the onion in the same oil until soft and lightly brown. Stir in the flour and cook for 1 minute.

❸ Crumble the Original Oxo cubes into 450 ml (¾ pint) boiling water. Gradually stir the stock into the onion. Bring to the boil and simmer for 1 minute.

❹ Return the meat to the pan. Cover and simmer slowly until the meat is tender – about 2 hours. Season with salt and pepper and stir in the parsley.

Place a pie funnel in a 1.1-litre (2-pint) pie dish. Add the meat and gravy to the dish and leave until completely cold.

❺ Preheat the oven to 200°C/400°F/Gas Mark 6.

❻ Roll out the pastry on a lightly floured surface. Place the pie dish on top of the pastry and cut a pastry lid 2.5 cm (1 inch) larger than the dish. Cut a 2.5 cm (1-inch) wide strip of pastry from the trimmings. Brush the lip of the pie dish with water and press the strip down all the way round it.

❼ Brush the strip with water and lay the pastry lid on top of the pie, pressing the edges firmly together. Trim off any excess pastry and flute the edge by pressing 2 fingers into the rim of the pastry and making small, even cuts between your fingers.

❽ Cut a small hole in the centre of the lid to allow the steam to escape. Cut some leaves from the pastry trimmings, dampen them and arrange them on the lid.

❾ Brush the pastry with beaten egg and bake for 30 minutes or until the pastry is well risen and golden.

Serves 4

Preparation time: 15–20 minutes + 2¾ hours cooking

Calories per serving 610

Tips

Make the filling a day ahead and pop it in the fridge overnight. This lets the flavours develop and speeds up your dinner preparations.

If the gravy looks too thin once it is cooked, remove the meat and boil the gravy vigorously in a saucepan until it reduces and thickens. Then pour it back over the meat and let everything cool completely.

If you like, you can omit the kidney and add 225 g (8 oz) sliced button mushrooms at the end of step 4 once the meat is cooked.

Microwave Tip

Transfer the ingredients to a microwave casserole after step 3. Cover the dish and cook on MEDIUM (50%) for about 1 hour, stirring often, until the meat is just tender. Transfer to the pie dish and continue as directed.

lamb chops with italian salsa
These chops would be great cooked on the barbecue. Be careful not to drip too much oil on to the coals as this could cause a flare-up.

2 Oxo Italian Herb and
Spice cubes

4 tablespoons olive oil

8 lamb chops

For the salsa

350 g (12 oz) tomatoes, skinned and diced

1 small onion, chopped finely

25 g (1 oz) pitted black or green olives, chopped finely

1 tablespoon lemon juice

1 tablespoon olive oil

salt and pepper

1 tablespoon chopped mint

❶ Crumble the Oxo Italian Herb and Spice cubes into the olive oil. Brush both sides of the chops with the seasoned oil and place them on a baking tray or grill pan.

❷ Put the diced tomatoes and chopped onion into a bowl with the olives, lemon juice and oil. Season with salt and pepper and stir in the mint.

❸ Preheat the grill and brush the chops again with the seasoned oil. Cook the chops under a medium-hot grill for about 5 minutes on each side (depending on their thickness), or until golden brown. Serve with the salsa.

Serves 4

Preparation and cooking time:
10–14 minutes

Calories per serving 470

Tip
In the summer try using plum tomatoes and red onions for the salsa.

pork chops in mustard
sauce Serve this elegant dish with fresh green vegetables such as beans or broccoli and new potatoes.

1 tablespoon sunflower or olive oil

15 g (¹/₂ oz) butter

4 boneless pork loin chops, with the fat trimmed

1 Original Oxo cube

2 teaspoons Dijon mustard

2 teaspoons cornflour

4 tablespoons single cream

1 tablespoon wholegrain mustard

salt and pepper

1 Heat the oil and butter in a frying pan and cook the chops over a medium heat for 20 minutes, turning once. Pour off any excess fat.

2 Crumble the Original Oxo cube into 300 ml (¹/₂ pint) boiling water and pour over the chops. Add the Dijon mustard. Cover and simmer for 10–15 minutes until the chops are tender.

3 Blend the cornflour with the cream, whisk into the pan with the wholegrain mustard. Simmer until thickened, season if necessary, and serve at once.

Serves 4

Preparation and cooking time: 35 minutes

Calories per serving 310

OXO Tip

For a treat you could cook rump steaks in the same way, frying them for 2 minutes on each side to seal them and then continuing as above.

sausage and mushroom crumble This casserole has
a delicious crispy topping.

2 tablespoons olive oil
450 g (1 lb) thick sausages
1 large onion, chopped
225 g (8 oz) button mushrooms
1–1½ tablespoons flour
1 Original Oxo cube
1 tablespoon tomato purée
salt and pepper

For the crumble topping
75 g (3 oz) butter
175 g (6 oz) plain flour
50 g (2 oz) grated Cheddar cheese
1 tablespoon chopped parsley

❶ Preheat the oven to 190°C/375°F/Gas Mark 5.
❷ Heat the oil in a large frying pan. Add the sausages and cook over a medium heat for about 5–6 minutes, until the sausages are browned all over. Take them out of the pan with tongs.
❸ Add the onion and cook for 4–5 minutes. Add the mushrooms and cook for 2 minutes. Stir in the flour.
❹ Crumble the Original Oxo cube into 300 ml (½ pint) boiling water. Stir into the mushrooms and onions and add the tomato purée.
❺ Cut each sausage into three pieces, return them to the pan and allow to simmer until the sauce thickens. Season if necessary and spoon into a shallow ovenproof dish.
❻ For the topping, rub the butter into the flour until it resembles fine breadcrumbs. Stir in the cheese and parsley, and sprinkle the mixture over the casserole.
❼ Bake for 40–45 minutes until golden.

Serves 4
Preparation time: 15 minutes + 45 minutes cooking
Calories per serving 675

Tip
Use good quality sausages for this dish.

Microwave Tip
Brown the sausages in a frying pan as directed. Place the oil and onion in a large microwave bowl and cook on HIGH (100%) for 2 minutes. Add the mushrooms and cook for 2 minutes more. Stir in the flour, stock and tomato purée. Cook for 5 minutes more, or until thickened. Transfer to an ovenproof dish, add the sausage pieces and continue from step 6.

Freezing Tip
Both the sausage and mushroom base and the crumble topping can be made ahead (prepared to the end of step 6), but freeze them separately. Thaw both thoroughly before assembling and cooking.

chinese pork kebabs with stir-fry vegetables This is another recipe which is ideal for cooking on the barbecue.

700 g (1½ lb) pork fillet, cut in 4 cm (1½-inch) cubes

For the marinade
2 Oxo Chinese Herb and Spice cubes
2 tablespoons sunflower oil
1 tablespoon soy sauce
2 tablespoons tomato ketchup

For the vegetables
100 g (4 oz) baby sweetcorn, halved lengthways
100 g (4 oz) mangetout
1 tablespoon sunflower oil
225 g (8 oz) beansprouts
1 Oxo Chinese Herb and Spice cube
2 tablespoons dry sherry

1 Put the cubed pork in a non-metallic bowl. Crumble 2 Oxo Chinese Herb and Spice cubes into a small bowl and add 1 tablespoon of boiling water. Stir. Add the oil, soy sauce and ketchup. Whisk together and pour the marinade over the pork. Cover and refrigerate for 2–4 hours.

2 Soak some bamboo skewers in water for 1 hour and then thread the pieces of marinated pork on to the skewers.

3 Preheat the grill. Cook the kebabs for 15–20 minutes, turning and brushing them with the marinade until the meat is tender.

4 Cook the sweetcorn for 3 minutes in boiling water, add the mangetout and cook for 1 minute more. Drain well.

5 Heat the oil in a frying pan, add the sweetcorn, mangetout and beansprouts. Crumble in the Oxo Herb and Spice cube, add the sherry and stir-fry for 2 minutes. The vegetables should still be crisp when served with the kebabs.

Serves 4
Preparation and cooking time: 20 minutes + 2–4 hours marinating
Calories per serving 380

Tips
This would be equally delicious with cubes of chicken breast.

Try threading diced red pepper or chopped pineapple chunks on to the skewers for extra colour and flavour.

It is important to soak bamboo skewers to stop them from scorching on the barbecue or under the grill.

Microwave Tip
Place the kebabs on a microwave roasting rack, cover with greaseproof paper and cook on MEDIUM (50%) for 10 minutes, turning the kebabs over half-way through. Wrap the kebabs in foil and let stand for 5 minutes.

pot roast beef

A flameproof casserole is a very useful article of kitchen equipment that allows you to brown meat before cooking it in the oven. However, if you do not have a flameproof casserole, you can sear the meat in a frying pan and then transfer it to an earthenware casserole.

2 tablespoons vegetable oil

1.1 kg (2 lb) brisket, boned and rolled

1 medium-size onion, chopped

2 large carrots, sliced thickly

2 large parsnips, sliced thickly

3 celery sticks, sliced thickly

2 Original Oxo cubes

150 ml (1/4 pint) red wine

1 bay leaf

1/2 teaspoon dried thyme

2 teaspoons cornflour

salt and pepper

1 Preheat the oven to 170°C/325°F/Gas Mark 3.

2 Heat the oil in a flameproof casserole. Add the brisket and sear until browned all over. Remove it from the pan.

3 Add the vegetables and cook gently for 3–4 minutes.

4 Place the meat on top of the vegetables.

5 Crumble the Original Oxo cubes into 600 ml (1 pint) boiling water and pour the stock over the meat. Pour in the wine and add the bay leaf and thyme.

6 Cover tightly and cook in the oven for 2 1/2 hours, or until the meat is tender when pierced with a fine skewer.

7 Remove the meat and place on a carving board.

8 Blend the cornflour with a little water and stir it into the meat juices. Simmer on the top of the stove until thickened, and season if necessary.

9 Carve the meat and serve with the vegetables and gravy.

Serves 4

Preparation time: 10 minutes + 2 1/2 hours cooking

Calories per serving 630

(OXO) **Tips**

If you wish to leave out the cornflour, push the vegetables through a sieve and mix them into the meat juices to make a tasty sauce.

Brisket is an exceptionally economical cut of meat and tastes wonderful if cooked slowly as in this recipe. You can sometimes find it on offer in supermarkets – if not your butcher will have it. Alternatively you could use topside of beef.

family beef casserole
Casseroles are so popular in cold weather that it is always worth making double and freezing some to have later.

3 tablespoons vegetable oil

900 g (2 lb) stewing steak, cut in 4 cm (1½-inch) cubes

2 medium-size onions, sliced thickly

3 large carrots, sliced thickly

3 medium-size parsnips, sliced thickly

2 tablespoons flour

2 Original Oxo cubes

1 tablespoon tomato purée

2 bay leaves

½ teaspoon dried thyme

salt and pepper

❶ Preheat the oven to 170°C/325°F/Gas Mark 3.

❷ Heat 2 tablespoons of the oil in a frying pan. Add the meat and fry until lightly browned. Transfer the meat to an ovenproof casserole using a slotted spoon.

❸ Add the rest of the oil to the pan. Stir in the vegetables and fry until lightly browned. Add them to the meat in the casserole.

❹ Stir the flour into the remaining juices in the frying pan.

❺ Crumble the Original Oxo cubes into 900 ml (1½ pints) of boiling water, and then add the stock to the frying pan. Stir in the tomato purée and simmer until smooth. Pour into the casserole.

❻ Add the herbs, cover and cook in the oven for 2–2¼ hours, or until the meat is tender. Add a little extra water if the gravy looks too thick. Stir once during cooking. Season if necessary and remove the bay leaves before serving.

Serves 4

Preparation time: 25 minutes + 2–2¼ hours cooking

Calories per serving 450

Tips
Try adding 25 g (1 oz) pearl barley for a slightly thicker stew.

Turnips would be a tasty alternative to parsnips.

❄ Freezing Tip
This casserole freezes very successfully. Cool quickly and pack into a container to freeze for up to 3 months.

barbecue burgers Use best-quality
lean mince to get the best results with this recipe.

700 g (1¹/₂ lb) extra lean
minced beef

1 small onion, chopped finely

2 Original Oxo cubes

2 tablespoons Worcestershire
sauce

2 tablespoons tomato ketchup

1 tablespoon mustard powder

4 soft hamburger rolls, halved

salad garnish to include crisp
lettuce leaves, sliced tomato,
onion rings and sliced dill
pickles

barbecue sauce, to taste

1 Mix together the minced
beef and finely chopped
onion in a bowl. Crumble
the Original Oxo cubes on
top.
2 Combine the
Worcestershire sauce,
ketchup and mustard
powder, add them to the
bowl and mix together
thoroughly.

3 Shape the mixture into
four round patties.
4 Prepare a barbecue, grill
or ridged frying pan to
cook the burgers. Brush the
rack or pan with a little oil
and cook the burgers for
6–8 minutes on each side.
5 Meanwhile, lightly toast
the cut halves of the rolls
and divide the salad garnish
between the four bottom
halves. Place a cooked patty
on each and add extra
barbecue sauce if desired.

Serves 4

Preparation and cooking time:
16 minutes

Calories per serving 530

Tips
Wet your hands between shaping
each patty if the mince is very
sticky.

Use a store-bought barbecue
sauce or make up some extra by
mixing 2 tablespoons each of
Worcestershire sauce and tomato
ketchup with 1 tablespoon of
mustard powder.

❄ Freezing Tip
Freeze the raw patties between
sheets of cling film. Thaw
completely before cooking.

cottage pie Cottage pie is always a firm family favourite, but this recipe has a slightly different topping.

2 tablespoons vegetable oil
700 g (1½ lb) minced beef
1 large onion, chopped
100 g (4 oz) mushrooms, quartered
1 tablespoon Worcestershire sauce
2 tomatoes, skinned and chopped, or 200 g (8 oz) canned tomatoes
½ teaspoon dried mixed herbs
2 Original Oxo cubes
700 g (1½ lb) small potatoes, peeled
50 g (2 oz) butter
2 teaspoons cornflour
salt and pepper

1 Heat a large frying pan until very hot. Add 1 tablespoon of oil. Add the minced beef and fry until the meat is browned, breaking up any large pieces with a wooden spoon. Transfer the meat to a saucepan.

2 Heat the rest of the oil in the frying pan, add the onion and cook for 3–4 minutes to soften. Add the mushrooms and cook for 2 minutes. Stir the onion and mushrooms into the minced beef with the Worcestershire sauce, tomatoes and dried herbs.
3 Crumble the Original Oxo cubes into 300 ml (½ pint) of boiling water. Pour the stock into the pan, cover and simmer for 40 minutes.
4 Preheat the oven to 200°C/400°F/Gas Mark 6.
5 Cut the potatoes into small, thin chips like thick matchsticks (they should be about 5 cm (2 inches) long and about 5 mm (¼ inch) thick. Melt the butter and toss the potatoes with the melted butter.
6 Blend the cornflour with a little water and stir it into the mince to thicken it. Season if necessary and spoon the mixture into a large ovenproof dish.
7 Place the chipped potatoes on top and bake for 40–45 minutes until crisp and golden.

Serves 4
Preparation and cooking time: 1¼–1½ hours
Calories per serving 640

Tip
For a more traditional cottage pie, boil 900 g (2 lb) potatoes until tender. Drain and mash with 50 g (2 oz) butter. Spread the mashed potato over the mince mixture and rough it up with a fork before baking.

Microwave Tip
Cook the onion and mushrooms with the oil in a large bowl on HIGH (100%) for 4–5 minutes. Add the minced beef and cook for 7–8 minutes more. Stir once to break up the mince. Stir in the tomatoes, Worcestershire sauce, stock and herbs. Cover and cook for 12 minutes more, stirring once. Thicken with the cornflour paste and continue with the recipe as directed.

Freezing Tip
The mince mixture can be made ahead (to the end of step 3), and then cooled and frozen until needed.

chilli con carne This famous Tex-Mex dish is inexpensive to make and ideal for an informal party. Serve in bowls with crusty bread or boiled rice.

1 tablespoon sunflower oil
1 large onion, chopped
450 g (1 lb) lean minced beef
1 Oxo Garlic, Herb and
Spice cube
2 teaspoons chilli powder
1 teaspoon ground coriander
1 teaspoon ground cumin
397 g can of chopped
tomatoes
3 tablespoons tomato purée
1 teaspoon dried oregano
1 Original Oxo cube
1 bay leaf
397 g can of red kidney beans
salt

① Heat the oil in a large frying pan with a lid. Add the onion and cook for 2–3 minutes until softened.
② Add the minced beef and cook over a high heat for 3–4 minutes. Break up any lumps with a wooden spoon as the mince browns.
③ Crumble in the Oxo Garlic, Herb and Spice cube. Add the chilli powder, ground coriander and ground cumin. Cook for 1 minute.
④ Stir in the chopped tomatoes, the tomato purée and the dried oregano. Crumble the Original Oxo cube into 300 ml ($^1/_2$ pint) boiling water and add to the pan with the bay leaf. Cover and simmer for 45 minutes.
⑤ Drain the kidney beans and add to the pan. Continue to cook for 15 minutes, seasoning with salt if necessary.

Serves 4

**Preparation and cooking time:
10 minutes + 1 hour cooking
Calories per serving 350**

Tip
An authentic Texan chilli contains braising steak cut in very small cubes, but this is time-consuming to prepare. Look out for coarse-cut minced beef.

Microwave Tip
Place the oil and onion in a large microwave dish, cover and cook on HIGH (100%) for 2 minutes. Add the minced beef and cook for 4 minutes longer, or until the meat is no longer pink. Stir in the rest of the ingredients (except for the beans) and cook for 8 minutes more. Add the beans, cook for 3 minutes more and then allow to stand for 5 minutes before serving.

Freezing Tip
Chilli con carne freezes well and will keep for up to 6 months.

poultry

all you need to know:
choosing & storing poultry

Poultry has become the most popular meat in Britain. Chicken and turkey are quick, versatile, easy to cook, and have the advantage of being interchangeable in most recipes. Duck is usually reserved for special occasions.

poultry and a healthy diet

Chicken and turkey are popular in part because they fit in so well with a healthy diet. High in protein and a good source of vitamin B, both are also low in fat, particularly when the skin is removed. Moreover the fat content of chicken and turkey is lower in saturated fats than most other meats.

choosing poultry

Most of the poultry available in this country is reared by intensive farming methods, which translates into affordable prices for chicken and turkey. However, free-range chicken and turkey, although more expensive, have a better flavour and are more succulent and tender.

A wide variety of poultry cuts is now available, both fresh and frozen. As well as whole birds, there are portions with and without skin and/or bone. You can also get chicken and turkey ready-diced, cut in strips for stir-frying, or minced, all of which are ideal for quick meals.

Whichever poultry cuts you choose, they should be as fresh as possible. Always buy poultry from a reputable shop – look for a well organised store with a rapid turnover. Check the 'use-by' date when buying from a supermarket. Look for the Quality British Chicken Mark on packaged birds. This indicates that the bird is grade 'A' and that it has been reared and produced according to standards set down for all stages of production. Check that the bird is firm and plump for its size and that the skin is not damaged or bruised. When judging the size of a bird allow at least 350 g (12 oz) per person.

storing and handing poultry

Poultry may contain low levels of the bacteria salmonella, listeria and campylobacter, which are potentially harmful and even life threatening. However, if poultry is stored and handled correctly, and cooked thoroughly, any bacteria will be killed by the heat and rendered harmless.

Get the poultry home (in a cool bag if possible) and into the fridge or freezer as soon after buying it as you are able. Remove the plastic wrapping and giblets and wrap the poultry loosely before refrigerating it in a shallow container. Store the giblets separately as they will deteriorate more rapidly.

To avoid cross-contamination, always wash your hands before and after preparing poultry. Never use the same utensils for preparing raw poultry and cooked foods. It's a good idea to keep one chopping board especially for preparing raw poultry. Eat fresh poultry as soon as possible and always within two days of purchase or according to the 'sell-by' date.

Frozen poultry will keep for up to three months. Make sure it is well wrapped to prevent freezer burn. To thaw poultry, puncture the wrappings and place it in the fridge, in a dish where the liquid won't drip on to any other food. Throw away the liquid once thawed. Defrost poultry thoroughly before cooking and cook it soon after thawing. Never re-freeze raw chicken or turkey. If poultry has been thawed in the microwave, it must be cooked immediately.

When defrosting a whole bird, check that there are no ice crystals left inside the cavity and that the legs and thighs are soft and pliable.

all you need to know:
types of poultry

chicken

Whole chickens: these are usually sold oven-ready, chilled or frozen with and without giblets; some butchers offer the giblets separately. Birds range in weight from 450 g (1 lb) up to 3.5 kg (7 lb). Allow at least 350 g (12 oz) per person. Whole chickens can be roasted, pot-roasted, poached or braised.

Poussins: these are very small chickens, 4–6 weeks old and weighing about 450 g (1 lb). One poussin serves 1–2 people. Poussins are tender but haven't a great deal of flavour, so they are best suited for barbecuing, frying or grilling, and served with a flavourful sauce.

Spring chickens: these are small birds, 12 weeks old and weighing about 1.1 kg (2½ lb). One spring chicken serves 2–3 people.

Corn-fed chickens: these have a distinctive yellow colour because they are reared on a diet of maize grain. This gives the flesh a better flavour. Corn-fed chickens are slightly more expensive and usually only available fresh. They are suitable for all types of cooking, but are best roasted, which makes the most of the flavour.

Free-range chickens: there is a variety of 'degrees' of free-range chickens which depends on the amount of space and open-air access they are given. They are always at least eight weeks old. Free-range birds have an excellent flavour and will work well in any dish.

turkey

Turkeys are now on sale all year round, in a range of sizes and portions.

Whole turkeys: these are sold fresh and frozen, ranging in size from 2.5 kg (5 lb) to as large as 13.5 kg (30 lb). All are oven-ready and some are self-basting, with butter or other fat inserted under the skin to keep the meat moist during cooking.

Small joints: for economical mid-week meals, small joints of turkey are cut from either breast or thigh meat; large breast portions are sold as small roasting joints.

Turkey joints: these include legs, thighs and breasts, with or without the bone.

Boneless turkey breasts: these are available as steaks, fillets and escalopes. They can be used in any recipe which calls for boneless chicken breasts. They're ideal for slicing thinly or cutting in strips for stir-frying.

Minced turkey: this is a low-fat alternative to minced beef, most often made from breast meat, but sometimes from the thigh and leg.

duck

Whole ducklings: these are available fresh or frozen and are best roasted.

Duck portions: these are becoming popular, particularly boneless breasts (sometimes known as *magrets*). Weighing about 225 g (8 oz) each, they can be roasted, pan-fried, sautéed or grilled. Sliced duck breasts are great for stir-fries.

jointing poultry

Chickens and turkeys of any size are tackled in exactly the same way. A sharp knife is essential – the heavier the better, so that you can exert more force. Special poultry shears make the job much easier although strong kitchen scissors can be used instead.

small birds

● Place the bird breast-side up and cut lengthways down and through the breastbone and then through the back-bone (see picture below).

● If necessary, divide in four by tucking the blade of the knife underneath the leg joint and slicing it away from the wing.

larger birds

● Hold the bird firmly on a board. Cut away the skin between the leg and breast, pull the leg away from the body and cut through between the thigh joint and the carcase (see picture below).

● Snap the bone away from the carcase and cut off the leg. Separate it into drumstick and thigh by cutting through the joint (see picture below). Repeat with the other leg.

● Cut down from the breast towards the wing joint, severing the wing (see picture below).

Fold the breast meat over the wing joint. Repeat with the other wing.
● Cut along the natural break in the rib cage, to separate the top of the breast from the lower carcase (see picture below).

Divide the breast into two or three pieces, depending on size.

all you need to know:
cooking poultry

stuffing

● Never stuff a bird in advance as bacteria in the uncooked bird may contaminate the stuffing. Make the stuffing, allow it to cool and then refrigerate it until just before cooking.

● Before stuffing, remove any giblets and rinse the bird inside and out, patting it dry with kitchen paper. Pull away any large lumps of fat from the vent end.

● Stuff the neck end only. Stuffing the body cavity slows down heat penetration, increasing the potential for an undercooked bird and a build up of bacteria in the cavity area.

● Do not pack the stuffing too tightly as it will expand during cooking.

● Tuck the flap of neck skin under, and either sew it in place or secure it with small skewers (see picture below).

Any excess stuffing can be cooked in an ovenproof dish or rolled into balls and placed round the bird during the last 30 minutes of roasting time.

easy steps for roasting birds

● Preheat the oven to the specified temperature.

● Remove the giblets. Rinse the bird under cold running water, drain it well and dry it thoroughly with kitchen paper, inside and out.

● If not using stuffing, place half a lemon or a small onion with some fresh herbs or garlic cloves in the bird's cavity. Alternatively, crumble in two Oxo Italian Herb and Spice or Oxo Garlic, Herb and Spice cubes.

● Truss the bird with fine string, folding the wings under the body and tying the legs together (see picture below).

Supermarket birds often come ready-trussed.

● Weigh the bird, including the stuffing, if any, and calculate the cooking time using the table on the right.

● Place the bird in a roasting tin, on a rack if you have one, season it with salt and pepper and smear the breast with butter or oil.

● You may prefer to cook whole birds in foil, which keeps the meat more moist, although it does tend to steam rather than to roast the bird. Take a wide roll of foil and fold it in half before placing it in the roasting tin. Put the bird in the tin and bring the edges of the foil up over it, to form a loose dome which encloses the bird completely (see picture below).

● Check the bird halfway through cooking and baste it with the roasting juices. If necessary, cover the breast loosely with a piece of foil to prevent it from browning too much. Conversely, if cooking in foil, open the dome and fold it back to allow the skin to brown.

● To test if the chicken or turkey is cooked, pierce the thickest part of the thigh with a skewer – if the juices run clear, it is done; if the juices are still pink, cook it longer. Allow the bird to stand for 15–25 minutes before carving.

Roasting temperatures and times

Poussin	200°C/400°F/Gas Mark 6	25–45 minutes in total
Chicken	200°C/400°F/Gas Mark 6	20 minutes per 450g (1 lb) + 20 minutes
Turkey	180°C/350°F/Gas Mark 4	
2.3–3.6 kg (5–8 lb)		without foil 2–2$^1/_2$ hours; with foil 2–2$^1/_2$ hours
3.6–5.0 kg (8–11 lb)		without foil 2$^1/_2$–3$^1/_4$ hours; with foil 3$^1/_4$–4 hours
5.0–6.8 kg (11–15 lb)		without foil 3$^1/_2$–3$^3/_4$ hours; with foil 4–5 hours
6.8–9.0 kg (15–20 lb)		without foil 3$^3/_4$–4$^1/_4$ hours; with foil 5–5$^1/_2$ hours
Duck	180°C/350°F/Gas Mark 4	30 minutes per 450g (1 lb)

making gravy for poultry

● Make up a stock using Chicken Oxo stock cubes.
● Pour off the fat from the roasting tin, leaving about 2 tablespoons of roasting juices. Pour in the Oxo stock, and stir vigorously to loosen any caramelised meat juices from the bottom of the tin.
● Blend 2 teaspoons of cornflour with a little water, and add to the gravy, stirring constantly until the gravy thickens.

carving poultry

You'll need a sharp, long-bladed carving knife and a carving fork.

● Put the bird on a board or large plate (a spiked carving dish is ideal) and let stand for 15–25 minutes.
● Remove any trussing strings or skewers.
● Holding the bird with the fork, cut the skin around the leg, insert

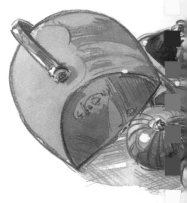

the knife between the leg and body and press gently to expose the joint (see picture below). Cut through and remove the thigh and drumstick.

● Remove the wing on the same side.
● Carve the breast meat downwards, parallel to the carcase (see picture below).

● Repeat on the other side.
● Carve turkey thighs parallel to the bone. Hold the drumsticks upright and carve them downwards.

pot-roasting chicken
● Choose a casserole with a tightly fitting lid.
● Brown the bird all over in butter and oil. Then cook it in its own juices, a little stock or wine, with vegetables such as onions, small potatoes and carrots.
● A variation of pot-roasting is to bake the poultry in a clay pot or 'chicken brick'. The pot is soaked in water beforehand so that the chicken stays moist during cooking.

grilling or barbecuing
Take care, when grilling poultry, as the intense heat tends to dry out the delicate meat. Marinating poultry beforehand helps (see page 13), as does basting with melted butter, oil and flavourings during cooking. Try crumbling different Oxo Herb and Spice cubes into the marinade to create fast and delicious grills. Marinate poultry for at least 2 hours before cooking, or leave it in the refrigerator overnight.

shallow-frying
This is ideal for chicken breasts and other small portions.

● Pat the joints dry with kitchen paper and shake them in a plastic bag with some seasoned flour. If you prefer a very crisp coating, dip the joints in beaten egg and roll them in seasoned breadcrumbs instead. You can add herbs and spices to the flour or breadcrumbs – or try crumbling in one or two Oxo Herb and Spice cubes.
● Heat some oil, or oil and butter, (butter alone will burn over a high heat) in a frying pan. Add the joints and fry over a high heat until the coating is sealed. Continue to cook over a medium heat until the meat is cooked through. Pierce the joints in their thickest point to check that the juices run clear, not pink.

deep-frying
Deep-frying is not suitable for cooking large poultry joints. It is ideal for cooking small pieces (nuggets) or strips of chicken or turkey.

● Coat the nuggets or strips in egg and seasoned flour or breadcrumbs as for shallow-frying.

● Fill a deep saucepan or deep-fryer one-third full of oil. Heat it to 185°C/ 360°F, or until a cube of day-old bread turns brown in one minute.
● Lower the coated poultry pieces into the oil using a wire basket, and cook for 3–5 minutes. Don't crowd the basket – it's better to cook two or more batches, reheating the oil between each batch (see picture below). Drain the nuggets or strips on kitchen paper and serve at once.

stir-frying
Stir-frying is a very quick and healthy way of cooking boneless chicken, turkey and duck. You can easily vary the seasonings by using different Oxo cubes to create a variety of fast and flavourful dishes.

● Make sure that the strips or chunks are of a similar size so that they cook evenly (see picture below).

● Prepare all of the ingredients in advance – once you begin stir-frying

you won't have time to chop vegetables and herbs.
● Heat a wok or large frying pan until a drop of oil sizzles on contact. Add 2 tablespoons of oil and heat until fairly hot.
● Add the meat and stir vigorously for 3–5 minutes, until the meat is cooked and browned all over.
● Generally speaking, it is a good idea to add the ingredients in order from slowest to fastest cooking – i.e. first the meat, then hard vegetables such as carrots, and finally softer vegetables such as mangetout. You can always remove the meat once it is cooked and re-heat it just before serving.

steaming
Steaming is a good way of cooking boneless poultry breasts and thighs without using oil or fat. The steaming liquid can be saved and added to a stock or soup.

● Remove the skin from the poultry and place the pieces in a steaming basket in a saucepan with a few inches of water in the bottom.
● Cover tightly and steam over a gentle heat for 20–25 minutes.

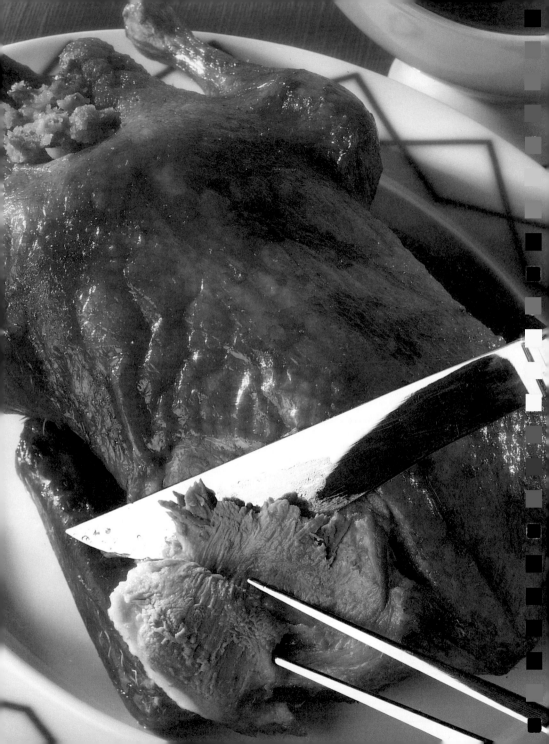

roast duck with mushroom and hazelnut stuffing

Duckling is sold both fresh and frozen, ready for the oven all year round. Do not buy a bird weighing less than 1.4 kg (3 lb) as there will be more bone than meat.

1.8–2.3 kg (4–5 lb) duckling

For the stuffing
25 g (1 oz) butter
50 g (2 oz) onion, chopped finely
100 g (4 oz) mushrooms, chopped finely
50 g (2 oz) toasted hazelnuts, chopped
2 Vegetable Oxo cubes
100 g (4 oz) fresh breadcrumbs
1 egg, beaten
salt and pepper

For the gravy
giblets
50 g (2 oz) onion
1 carrot, sliced
1 Chicken Oxo cube
1 tablespoon flour

❶ Remove the giblets from the cavity of the duck and set aside.
❷ Wash the duck inside and out and pat dry with kitchen paper. Remove any fat from inside the cavity. Preheat the oven to 180°C/350°F/Gas Mark 4.
❸ To make the stuffing, melt the butter in a frying pan, add the onion and mushrooms and cook for 3–4 minutes until softened. Put in a bowl and add the hazelnuts, crumbled Vegetable Oxo cubes and the breadcrumbs. Add the beaten egg, season and mix together well.
❹ Fill the cavity with the stuffing and then turn the parson's nose inside to form a closure. Weigh the duck and calculate the roasting time (page 41).
❺ Prick the skin all over with a fork to encourage the fat to run. Sprinkle a little salt over the breast. Place the duck, breast-side up, on a rack in a roasting tin
❻ Cook until crisp and golden all over. During cooking a lot of fat will come out of the duck. Drain this off twice – otherwise it can get smoky in the oven. Brush a little of this fat over the skin.
❼ Wash the giblets and put them into a pan with the whole onion. Add the carrot and 600 ml (1 pint) cold water. Slowly bring to the boil and skim off any scum which rises to the surface. Crumble in the Chicken Oxo cube. Allow to simmer gently for 1½ hours.
❽ Strain the stock and (if necessary) boil vigorously until it is reduced to 300 ml (½ pint).
❾ Lift the duck on to a warm serving plate. Pour off as much fat as possible from the roasting tin and stir the flour into the remaining juices. Gradually stir in the reduced stock. Simmer on top of the stove for 3–4 minutes until thickened. Season if necessary, and then strain into a gravy jug.

Serves 4
Preparation time: 20 minutes + 2 hours cooking
Calories per serving 530

Tip
Duck can be a fatty meat, but if you roast it as suggested here, you will get rid of a lot of the fat. To reduce the fat content further, remove the skin before eating.

country chicken soup This is an excellent recipe to use up leftover chicken.

1 tablespoon oil

1 small onion, finely chopped

2 small leeks, sliced

1 medium-size carrot, chopped

1 medium-size courgette, chopped

1 tablespoon flour

2 Chicken Oxo cubes

100 g (4 oz) cooked chicken, shredded

salt and pepper

❶ Heat the oil in a large saucepan. Add the onion and cook gently for 5 minutes until softened.
❷ Add the rest of the vegetables, cover and cook for 2 minutes more. Stir in the flour.
❸ Crumble the Chicken Oxo cubes into 900 ml (1½ pints) boiling water. Pour into the pan and bring to the simmer.
❹ Simmer gently for 15 minutes, or until the vegetables are tender. Stir in the chicken, cook for 2 minutes more and then season if necessary.

Serves 4

Preparation and cooking time: 30 minutes

Calories per serving 110

Tip

Substitute cooked turkey for the chicken.

Microwave Tip

Place the oil and onion in a large bowl, cover and cook on HIGH (100%) for 3 minutes. Stir in the vegetables and cook for 2 minutes more. Add the flour and the stock and cook for 7 minutes. Stir in the chicken and cook for 3–5 minutes more.

orange chicken stir-fry
Stir-fries are so quick to cook and make ideal dishes for midweek meals. Serve with noodles.

1 tablespoon vegetable oil

75 g (3 oz) cashew nuts

450 g (1 lb) skinless chicken breast fillet, cut in finger-length strips

1 large carrot, cut in matchsticks

175 g (6 oz) broccoli florets

100 g (4 oz) mangetout

3 Oxo Chinese Herb and Spice cubes

zest of 1/2 orange

juice of 1 large orange

1/2 teaspoon cornflour

4 spring onions, green tips only, sliced

1 Heat the oil in a large frying pan or wok. Add the cashew nuts and cook until lightly browned. Remove from the pan using a slotted spoon and drain on kitchen paper.

2 Re-heat the pan. Add the chicken and cook over a high heat until lightly browned.

3 Add the carrot, broccoli and mangetout. Crumble in the Oxo Chinese Herb and Spice cubes and add the orange zest. Stir-fry for 3–4 minutes.

4 Blend the orange juice with the cornflour. Add to the pan with the cashew nuts and cook for 1 minute.

5 Scatter the spring onions over the top and serve at once.

Serves 4

Preparation and cooking time: 10 minutes

Calories per serving 330

OXO Tip

Stir-fries can be adapted easily to make vegetarian dishes. Leave out the chicken and add more vegetables such as thin strips of celery, thickly sliced water chestnuts, or thickly sliced mushrooms.

sweet and spicy chicken
This is the perfect dish for when you get home and find only some chicken breasts in the fridge. All it needs is some crusty bread and a salad.

zest and juice of 1 lime

4 tablespoons apricot jam, warmed

1 Oxo Garlic, Herb and Spice cube

1 teaspoon cayenne pepper

1 teaspoon paprika

4 boneless, skinless chicken breasts

1 Preheat the oven to 200°C/400°F/Gas Mark 6.

2 Stir together the lime zest and juice with the apricot jam in a small bowl. Crumble in the Oxo Garlic, Herb and Spice cube. Add the spices.

3 Line an ovenproof dish with foil. Arrange the chicken breasts in it and spread them with the spicy jam glaze. Cook for 25–30 minutes, basting with the glaze 2 or 3 times during cooking.

Serves 4

Preparation and cooking time: 25–30 minutes

Calories per serving 190

Tip

Line the dish with foil or you will have a very sticky dish to wash! Bastes and glazes containing jam, sugar or honey will bake on to dishes and burn around the edges.

american chicken pie This is
a lovely family recipe with an intriguing topping.

4 x 175 g (6 oz) boneless,
skinless chicken breasts

2 medium-size carrots, sliced

1 Chicken Oxo cube

25 g (1 oz) butter

1 small onion, chopped finely

100 g (4 oz) rindless, smoked
back bacon, cut in 1 cm
(1/2-inch) pieces

200 g (7 oz) canned sweetcorn,
drained

2 tablespoons flour

150 ml (1/4 pint) milk

5 tablespoons crème fraîche
or double cream

2 tablespoons chopped parsley

salt and pepper

For the topping

1 Oxo Italian Herb and
Spice cube

50 g (2 oz) butter, slightly
softened

2 bagels

50 g (2 oz) Cheddar cheese,
grated

❶ Place the chicken breasts and carrots in a shallow pan or frying pan. Crumble the Chicken Oxo cube into 450 ml (3/4 pint) boiling water. Pour into the pan and bring back to the boil. Cover and simmer gently for 20 minutes.

❷ Remove the chicken and carrots from the pan using a slotted spoon and boil the liquor vigorously until it is reduced to 300 ml (1/2 pint) – this will concentrate its flavour. Pour into a jug and set aside.

❸ Cut the chicken into bite-size pieces and place it in a large bowl with the carrots.

❹ Preheat the oven to 190°C/375°F/Gas Mark 5.

❺ Melt the butter and sauté the onion and bacon for 3–4 minutes until golden. Remove with a slotted spoon and add to the chicken along with the sweetcorn.

❻ Stir the flour into the butter in the pan and cook over a low heat for 1 minute. Remove from the heat and gradually add the reserved stock and milk. Cook over a medium heat, whisking until smooth and thickened.

❼ Add the crème fraîche or cream and parsley to the sauce. Season if necessary and add the sauce to the bowl with the chicken. Fold everything together and transfer to a large, shallow ovenproof dish.

❽ For the topping, crumble the Oxo Italian Herb and Spice cube and mix it in with the butter. Slice each bagel in 4 thin slices and toast until pale golden. Spread with the savoury butter and arrange over the chicken filling. Scatter the cheese over the top.

❾ Bake for 25–30 minutes or until crisp and golden.

Serves 4
Preparation time: 30 minutes + 30 minutes cooking
Calories per serving 750

Tip
You can make this pie successfully with cooked chicken or turkey. Make the stock with 300 ml (1/2 pint) water and cook the carrots until tender.

Freezing Tip
The pie filling can be made in advance and frozen. Thaw it thoroughly before adding the bagel topping and baking.

cheesy stuffed chicken
This chicken dish is crisp and crunchy with a great combination of flavours.

4 boneless, skinless chicken breasts

2 Oxo Garlic, Herb and Spice cubes

100 g (4 oz) cream cheese

1 tablespoon chopped parsley

2 Oxo Italian Herb and Spice cubes

75 g (3 oz) fresh breadcrumbs

25 g (1 oz) grated parmesan cheese

1 large egg, beaten

❶ Cut a slit lengthways in each chicken breast. Don't cut right through – you want to create a pocket in each breast. Preheat the oven to 190°C/375°F/Gas Mark 5.

❷ Crumble the Oxo Garlic, Herb and Spice cubes into the cream cheese. Add the parsley and mix well. Fill each pocket with the mixture and then press the cut edges back together. ❸ Crumble the Oxo Italian Herb and Spice cubes and mix together with the breadcrumbs and parmesan cheese. Spread this mixture on a plate. ❹ Dip each chicken breast in the beaten egg and then in the breadcrumbs. (Use two forks for easy handling.) ❺ Put the chicken in a roasting tin and cook for 30 minutes, or until golden and crisp.

Serves 4

Preparation time: 15 minutes + 30 minutes cooking

Calories per serving 400

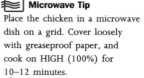 **Tips**

Instead of the breadcrumb coating, you could wrap each chicken breast in ham, bacon or Parma ham. Braise the parcels in a little chicken stock in the oven.

If you have any breadcrumb mixture left over, you can freeze it and sprinkle it on top of any oven bake before cooking.

Microwave Tip

Place the chicken in a microwave dish on a grid. Cover loosely with greaseproof paper, and cook on HIGH (100%) for 10–12 minutes.

Freezing Tip

You can prepare the chicken in advance (up to the end of step 4). Then either store in the refrigerator for a couple of hours until needed or freeze, making sure to thaw it thoroughly before cooking.

mediterranean chicken
casserole You could joint a whole
chicken for this dish (see page 39) or buy
portions from the butcher or supermarket.

2 tablespoons olive oil

1.6 kg (3¹/₂ lb) chicken,
cut in 8 pieces

1 large Spanish onion, sliced

1 red pepper, deseeded
and sliced

1 yellow pepper, deseeded
and sliced

4 ripe tomatoes, skinned
and chopped roughly

1 tablespoon tomato purée
(optional)

1 Chicken Oxo cube

2 Oxo Garlic, Herb and
Spice cubes

2 teaspoons cornflour

salt and pepper

chopped parsley, to garnish

1 Heat the oil in a large flameproof casserole. Add the chicken pieces and cook until golden brown. Remove from the pan.

2 Add the onion to the pan and cook for 5 minutes until golden. Then add the peppers and cook for 2–3 minutes. Add the tomatoes and tomato purée (if using).

3 Crumble the Chicken Oxo cube into 300 ml (¹/₂ pint) of boiling water. Pour the stock into the pan and crumble in the Oxo Garlic, Herb and Spice cubes. Return the chicken to the pan, bring to a boil and then cover and simmer for 45 minutes.

4 Blend the cornflour with 1 tablespoon of water. Stir into the casserole and simmer until thickened. Season if necessary.

5 Scatter the parsley over the top and serve.

Serves 4

Preparation time: 20 minutes
+ 45 minutes cooking

Calories per serving 400

Tip
You can reduce the fat content of this dish by removing the skin from the chicken before you cook it.

Microwave Tip
Brown the chicken in a frying pan. Soften the oil and onion in a shallow microwave dish on HIGH (100%) for 2 minutes. Add the peppers and cook for 3 minutes more. Stir in the browned chicken along with the remaining ingredients and cook on HIGH (100%) for 18–20 minutes, or until the chicken is tender.

Freezing Tip
Prepare the casserole up to the end of step 3 and freeze. Use within 3 months.

quick chicken curry This curry is made Balti-style, which means the ingredients are stir-fried. Serve with boiled basmati rice and poppadoms.

2 tablespoons vegetable oil

2 medium-size onions, sliced

450 g (1 lb) boneless, skinless chicken breasts, cut in bite-size pieces

1 red pepper, deseeded and cut in chunks

1 green pepper, deseeded and cut in chunks

1 garlic clove, crushed or 1 Oxo Garlic, Herb and Spice cube

3 Oxo Indian Herb and Spice cubes

1 Chicken Oxo cube

150 ml (1/4 pint) natural yogurt

1 teaspoon cornflour

salt and pepper

1 Heat the oil in a frying pan with a lid. Add the onions and cook for 5–6 minutes until golden.

2 Add the chicken pieces and stir-fry for 5–6 minutes until the chicken and onions are lightly brown.

3 Add the peppers, crushed garlic or crumbled Oxo Garlic, Herb and Spice cube, and crumble in the three Oxo Indian Herb and Spice cubes. Cook over a medium heat for 3 minutes.

4 Crumble the Chicken Oxo cube into 150 ml (1/4 pint) boiling water. Pour into the pan and stir. Bring to a boil and then cover the pan and simmer for 5 minutes.

5 Meanwhile, blend the yogurt and cornflour together. Stir into the pan and simmer for 5 minutes. Season if necessary.

Serves 4

Preparation and cooking time: 25 minutes

Calories per serving 260

Tips

You can adapt this dish to make a quick Balti lamb curry. Choose a tender cut such as neck fillet. You will need to simmer the dish in step 4 for about 15 minutes extra.

If you don't have a frying pan with a lid, use a baking tray or some kitchen foil to cover the pan.

chicken in a pot This method of cooking keeps the chicken very succulent and gives it a good flavour.

1.6 kg (3¹/₂ lb) oven-ready chicken

1 medium-size onion, halved

1 tablespoon oil

15 g (¹/₂ oz) butter

1 Chicken Oxo cube

225 g (8 oz) baby carrots

225 g (8 oz) baby turnips

2 tablespoons chopped parsley

2 tablespoons cornflour (optional)

① Wipe the chicken with damp kitchen paper and stuff the cavity with the onion halves.

② Preheat the oven to 180°C/350°F/Gas Mark 4.

③ Heat the oil and butter in a flameproof casserole and cook the chicken, turning until browned all over.

④ Crumble the Chicken Oxo cube into 300 ml (¹/₂ pint) boiling water. Pour the stock over the chicken and place the carrots and turnips around it.

⑤ Cover the casserole tightly and cook in the oven for 1¹/₂ hours or until the chicken is tender.

⑥ Lift the chicken on to a serving dish. Surround with the vegetables and scatter with parsley.

⑦ If you like, you can thicken the cooking juices with the cornflour blended with a little water.

Serves 4

Preparation time: 10 minutes + 1³/₄ hours cooking

Calories per serving 380

Tips

If you can't find baby vegetables in the shops, use larger ones cut in chunks.

You may wish to serve this dish with extra vegetables (such as potatoes and peas) or to turn it into a one-pot meal. If so, double the quantity of carrots and turnips.

garlic turkey sausages
These turkey sausages are a great barbecue recipe – or they can be pan-fried or baked in the oven. Serve with a leafy green salad.

25 g (1 oz) fresh white
breadcrumbs

2 Oxo Garlic, Herb and
Spice cubes

450 g (1 lb) minced turkey

225 g (8 oz) sausagemeat

1 small egg, beaten

salt and pepper

a little oil

1 Put the breadcrumbs in a bowl. Crumble in the Oxo Garlic, Herb and Spice cubes and mix together.

2 Add the rest of the ingredients (except for the oil) and mix together thoroughly.

3 Divide in 12 balls. Form the mixture into sausage shapes about 10 cm (4 inches) long, wetting your hands often. Place them on a baking tray and refrigerate for at least 30 minutes.

4 Preheat the grill. Brush the grill pan and sausages with oil. Cook for 20 minutes, turning them frequently, until golden brown all over.

Serves 4

Preparation time: 10 minutes + 30 minutes chilling + 20 minutes cooking

Calories per serving 300

Tip
Use a food processor to make a large quantity of breadcrumbs and freeze the extra in plastic freezer bags.

Microwave Tip
Place the sausages on a microwave rack in a baking dish and cook on HIGH (100%) for 8 minutes, turning the sausages and rotating the baking dish half-way through cooking.

Freezing Tip
You can make the sausages ahead and freeze them. Thaw thoroughly before cooking.

mexican turkey salad
This delicious salad is just perfect for picnics.

75 g (3 oz) long-grain rice

450 g (1 lb) turkey breast,
cut in thin strips

3 tablespoons olive oil

2 Oxo Garlic, Herb and
Spice cubes

1–1$\frac{1}{2}$ teaspoons chilli powder

1 teaspoon paprika

1 red pepper, deseeded
and diced

$\frac{1}{2}$ medium-size red onion or
6 spring onions, sliced finely

397 g can of red kidney beans,
drained and rinsed

1 medium-size avocado

2 tablespoons lemon or
lime juice

50 g (2 oz) grated Cheddar
or Monterey Jack cheese

taco or tortilla chips, to serve

1 Cook the rice in slightly salted water for about 10–12 minutes until tender. Drain and rinse in cold water, and then drain again. Place in a large bowl.

2 Put the turkey strips in another bowl. Add the oil and crumble in the Oxo Garlic, Herb and Spice cubes, chilli powder to taste and paprika. Mix thoroughly and marinate for 30 minutes.

3 Heat a frying pan and add the turkey and seasoned oil. Stir-fry for 5–6 minutes until cooked. Add to the rice and allow to cool.

4 Add the pepper, onion or spring onions and kidney beans to the rice mixture.

5 Halve the avocado, discard the stone and remove the peel. Cut the flesh in small pieces and toss them in the lemon or lime juice. Gently fold them into the salad.

6 Turn into a shallow dish and scatter the cheese and taco or tortilla chips around the edge.

Serves 4

Preparation and cooking time:
20 minutes + 30 minutes
marinating

Calories per serving 630

Tips
You can prepare the salad in advance up to the end of step 4. Cover and store in the fridge until you are ready to serve it.

No dressing is necessary as the oil and lemon juice are sufficient to flavour and moisten the salad.

fish

all you need to know:
choosing & storing fish

Versatile, quick and easy to cook, fish is very much the food of today. Fish lends itself to all types of cooking and can be made into meals and snacks for all occasions.

fish and a healthy diet

Fish is highly nutritious, providing essential protein, B vitamins, and minerals such as iodine and calcium. Oily fish such as salmon, mackerel, tuna and sardines also provide vitamins A and D. The fat contained in oily fish is mainly polyunsaturated — the Omega-3 fatty acids, in particular, are said to help prevent heart disease. It is recommended that everyone eats oily fish once a week.

choosing fish

Whether you buy your fish from the supermarket or from a fishmonger, the shop should smell fresh and all surfaces and display areas look clean. The fish should be displayed on ice, or on trays at a temperature just above freezing.

All fresh fish should look moist and have a clean, mild smell. Whole fish should have clear, bright eyes, bright red or pink gills, and shiny, undamaged skin. Fish fillets and steaks should be firm and moist, showing no signs of dryness or discolouration. Do not buy fish which has a strong, 'fishy' smell.

For maximum flavour and goodness, eat fresh fish on the day of purchase. Shellfish, in particular, should be eaten very fresh. They should have a clean, sea smell and look bright and moist.

Do not overlook the advantages of frozen fish. Almost every type of fish can be bought frozen all year round and the price will often be lower than that of fresh fish.

A good fishmonger or supermarket fish counter will prepare the fish to your requirements, so you can get them to gut, clean, scale, fillet and even skin it for you. Pre-packed fish from supermarkets is usually ready to cook, requiring little in the way of preparation or handling. Anyone who dislikes eating fish because of bones should look out for ready-filleted, de-boned fish, in particular.

A fish that has been cut into steaks or fillets deteriorates more rapidly than a whole fish, so it is often wise to choose a whole fish from the fishmonger and then ask him to prepare it.

storing fish

Once purchased, fish should be refrigerated as soon as possible and eaten on the same day. If you can't cook the fish on the day of purchase, rinse it in cold water, pat it dry with kitchen paper, and cover and store it in the coldest part of your refrigerator. It will keep safely for 24 hours. You can only keep it for longer intervals when frozen, and then only if it hasn't been frozen previously (ask when you buy). Do not re-freeze fish once it has been thawed. Oily fish can be frozen for up to three months, but, for the best flavour, use it before 1–2 months. White fish can be kept for up to six months in the freezer.

It is best to thaw fish slowly in the refrigerator before cooking it. Fillets that are not too thick can be cooked from frozen.

all you need to know:
types of fish

white fish

There is a wide variety of white fish, most of which are suitable for all types of cooking. White fish can be divided into two families, round and flat fish.

round fish

cod: this flaky fish is sold as fillets, steaks and cutlets. It's one of the most popular of all fish, and has a clear, firm, white flesh. Codling is a small version of cod.

haddock: similar in flavour to cod, haddock is usually sold filleted, although occasionally small whole fish are available. The flesh separates easily into large flakes.

hake: this long, thin fish has a good flavour and is available as steaks.

coley: also known as saithe, coley has a slightly greyish-pink colour, but turns completely white when cooked. It's very economical and useful for making fish cakes and pies.

whiting: related to cod, whiting is less expensive and has a firm, sweet flesh.

flat fish

plaice: a popular white fish with a good flavour and fine texture, plaice is sold whole or as fillets and is suitable for all types of cooking. It responds well to flavoured sauces. Plaice can be used as a substitute for sole fillets.

lemon sole: skinned and filleted, lemon sole lends itself well to rich sauces.

dover sole: one of the finest fish in flavour and texture, Dover sole is best served plainly grilled with lemon juice and butter.

skate: this is a large flat fish, of which only the wings are used. It's best floured and shallow-fried or poached.

coley

cod

skate

whiting

hake

dover sole

haddock

whiting

lemon sole

plaice

oily fish

herring, sprats, sardines and whitebait: all of these belong to the same family. Good value for money, these fish have a rich flavour and are highly nutritious. They are excellent fried, grilled or barbecued.

mackerel: an increasingly popular fish, mackerel combines the richness of herring but with a much firmer flesh. It's sold whole or as fillets, and should be grilled, fried or baked.

tuna: increasingly available as steaks, fresh tuna is excellent for grilling and barbecuing.

freshwater fish

Freshwater fish can still be caught in rivers and lakes, but these days they are often farmed. Farmed fish are less expensive than those caught in the wild, and they are readily available all year.

salmon: wild salmon is available seasonally but tends to be expensive. Farmed salmon is sold whole or cut in steaks, boned fillets and cutlets. Salmon is suitable for poaching, grilling, baking or barbecuing, and is one of the few fish which can be poached and then served cold.

trout: a delicately flavoured fish which can be cooked whole or in fillets, trout is very versatile and responds to most methods of cooking apart from deep-frying.

smoked fish

Smoking is a traditional way of preserving fish. Smoked salmon is considered a luxury, but the less expensive smoked fish, such as trout, kippers and mackerel, make equally delicious meals.

smoked haddock: also known as Finnan haddock, fillets of smoked haddock are often dyed to look deep golden but, left in their natural state, they will be pale in colour. Smoked haddock is best poached with a little milk, either on the hob or in the oven. Smoked cod fillets can be cooked in the same way.

shellfish

Shellfish include a wide variety of seafood, the most popular being prawns, which are now available in different sizes.

north atlantic prawns: these are usually sold cooked and frozen, with and without shells.

mediterranean prawns: these are large prawns also known as king prawns.

tiger prawns: imported from south-east Asia, these prawns are often used in oriental dishes.

mussels (below): these are relatively inexpensive shellfish, sold raw (live) in their shells, or cooked and without their shells.

Other readily available shellfish include crabs, lobsters, scallops, scampi (Dublin Bay prawns), squid and shrimps.

tiger prawns

mediterranean prawns

north atlantic prawns

squid

mackerel

sardines

sprats

herring

trout

tuna

sprats

salmon

undyed smoked haddock

dyed smoked haddock

all you need to know:
preparing fish

scoring fish

Score whole fish that are to be grilled, baked or steamed, so that they cook more evenly. Scoring also prevents the skin from bursting during cooking. Using a sharp knife, make 3–4 diagonal slashes on each side of the fish (see picture below).

filleting a round fish (e.g., trout)

● Place the fish flat on a board and cut along its belly (see picture below).

● Starting at the head end, cut along the centre of the back. Ease the flesh away from the bone using short, sharp strokes (see picture below). Remove the fillet from the other side in the same way.

boning a round fish to leave whole

● Remove the head and split the fish down the belly (see picture below).

● Turn the fish over, skin-side up, and press firmly down the centre of the fish along its length (see picture below).

● Turn the fish over again – the back bone should lift off easily (see picture below).

Cut the bone off at the tail using scissors. This technique is particularly effective for herring or mackerel, especially if they are to be stuffed.

filleting a flat fish into 4 fillets (e.g., plaice)

Two or four fillets can be taken from a flat fish.
● Using scissors, cut off both fins.
● Place the fish on a board, dark-side up. Using a sharp knife, cut down the centre and around the head (see picture below).

● Slide the knife under one fish fillet, and loosen it from the spine at the head end. Slice the flesh away from the spine, keeping the knife as close to the bone as possible (see picture below). Repeat with the three other fillets.

● Rub the fish with salt to remove any dark patches. Rinse well under cold water and then pat dry with kitchen paper.

skinning fillets

● Hold the fillet firmly by the tail (use a little salt to get a good grip) and insert the knife under the skin at the tail end of the fillet. Press the knife's blade at an angle along the skin, and ease the flesh away (see picture below).

all you need to know:
cooking fish

Fish cooks quickly, so it is important to keep an eye on it. When cooked, fish will be firm and opaque. Its flesh will stay together but flake easily. Using the tip of a knife, gently prod the fish at its thickest part to check whether it is cooked through.

poaching

White fish, smoked fish, salmon fillets, fish steaks and whole fish can all be poached successfully either on the hob or in the oven at 180°C/350°F/Gas Mark 4.

● Place the fish in a pan with a tight-fitting lid and pour in enough liquid to half cover the fish. Use seasoned water, wine, cider or milk.
● Bring the liquid to a bare simmer and cook until the fish is firm and opaque. Allow 6–8 minutes for a 175–200 g (6–7 oz) steak or fillet. Whole fish may take up to 10 minutes.
● If poaching fish to serve cold, bring the liquid just to the boil and then turn the heat off and leave the fish until cool.
● Reduce the poaching liquid to make a sauce, or freeze it for soup stock.

steaming

Steaming is an excellent method of cooking fillets and small whole fish without using fat.

● Bring about 5 cm (2 inches) of water to a simmer in a saucepan.
● Place the prepared fish in the steamer and fit it into the saucepan, covering it with a tightly-fitting lid.
● Steam for 5–8 minutes for small fillets or 8–10 minutes for steaks and whole fish weighing up to 200 g (7 oz). Larger fish (up to 350 g/12 oz) will take from 10–15 minutes. The fish is ready when it is opaque, firm to the touch and flakes easily.

shallow-frying

This is suitable for fillets, steaks and whole fish.

● Pat the fish dry with kitchen paper and coat it with either seasoned flour or with beaten egg and breadcrumbs. (See page 76 for more detail.)
● Use a frying pan large

● Heat the oil to 190°C/375°F, or until a small cube of day-old bread turns golden brown in 60 seconds.
● Lower the pieces of fish into the oil and cook until the batter is golden and crisp, by which time the fish will be cooked inside.
● Lift the fish out of the pan on to crumpled kitchen paper, to drain.
● Small strips of fish called goujons, coated in seasoned flour, beaten egg and then breadcrumbs, can be deep-fried in 2–3 minutes.

grilling
Both whole fish and fillets or steaks can be grilled. Many kinds of fish can also be barbecued – whole fish can be placed on the rack but more delicate pieces of fish are safer wrapped in foil. Special fish-shaped holders are available which make barbecuing very easy.

● Line the grill pan with foil and heat the grill to high for small pieces of fish and medium for larger, whole fish.
● Have oil or melted butter on hand to brush the fish – this will prevent it from drying out. Brush the underside of the fish to stop it from sticking to the rack.
● Cooking times will depend on the size of the fish and the heat of the

grill. Thin fillets will not need turning but you should turn thick fillets and whole fish once during cooking. The fish is ready when it is firm to the touch and the flesh is opaque.

baking
● Place the prepared fish in a buttered ovenproof dish, or wrap individual pieces in foil.
● Season the fish with a sprinkling of an Oxo Herb and Spice cube, dot with butter, cover (or wrap) and cook at 180°C/350°F/Gas Mark 4 for 20–30 minutes.
● Thick fish fillets or boned steaks can be roasted with a topping or stuffing. In this case, cook at 190°C/375°F/Gas Mark 5, and uncover for the last few minutes of cooking to allow the topping to get crispy.

microwaving
Fish cooks well in the microwave. Small whole fish, cutlets, steaks and fillets are all suitable. Always cover the fish and use less liquid than for conventional cooking. Arrange the thinnest part of the fish towards the middle of the dish. The cooking time will depend on the power of the cooker, so refer to the manufacturer's handbook.

enough to hold the fish and heat enough oil, or oil and butter, to coat the base of the pan evenly.
● When fairly hot, add the prepared fish. Cook larger whole fish for 4–6 minutes on each side, and smaller fillets for 2–3 minutes per side. Use a fish slice or palette knife to turn the fish over.
● Drain fish coated with breadcrumbs on kitchen paper before serving.

deep-frying
You'll need a wide, heavy pan filled one-third full with groundnut oil. If the pan contains too much oil, there is a real danger of it bubbling over. Have the fish prepared and ready to be dipped into the batter (see page 83 for batter recipe).

fish and potato pie For a special occasion use a mixture of white fish and salmon, or add some peeled prawns.

1 Vegetable Oxo cube

700 g (1¹/₂ lb) cod or haddock fillet, skinned

25 g (1 oz) butter

2 tablespoons flour

300 ml (¹/₂ pint) milk

2 tablespoons chopped parsley

400 g packet potato rosti

salt and pepper

❶ Preheat the oven to 190°C/375°F/Gas Mark 5.
❷ Crumble the Vegetable Oxo cube into a frying pan with 300 ml (¹/₂ pint) water. Bring to the boil. Add the fish to the pan, cover and simmer gently for 6–8 minutes until just cooked.
❸ Lift the fish out of the pan, drain and place in a shallow ovenproof dish. Discard any visible bones.
❹ Return the pan to full heat and boil vigorously until the stock is reduced to 150 ml (¹/₄ pint).
❺ Melt the butter in a saucepan, stir in the flour and cook for 1 minute over a low heat. Gradually add the milk and the reduced stock. Bring back to a simmer, stirring all the time until thick and smooth. Season and add the parsley.
❻ Pour the sauce over the fish. Fold together gently and level the surface. Crumble the potato rosti over the top and bake for 30 minutes, or until golden.

Serves 4

Preparation time: 10 minutes + 40–45 minutes cooking

Calories per serving 410

Tip
Potato rosti is a grated potato mixture which is normally fried. It can be bought in packets and has a long shelf-life, making it an ideal quick potato topping. If you prefer, use mashed potato instead.

Microwave Tip
Place the fish in a microwave dish with the stock. Cover and cook for 4–5 minutes on HIGH (100%) until just cooked.

Freezing Tip
You can prepare the fish and sauce filling ahead and freeze it. Defrost thoroughly, add the potato topping and bake.

seafood stew Serve this in shallow bowls and have plenty of crusty bread on hand to mop up the juices. You can use haddock or hoki instead of cod if you prefer.

2 tablespoons olive oil

1 small onion, chopped

1 garlic clove, crushed or
1 Oxo Garlic, Herb and
Spice cube

1 red pepper, deseeded
and chopped

397 g can of chopped
tomatoes

2 Oxo Italian Herb and
Spice cubes

150 ml (¼ pint) dry white wine

450 g (1 lb) cod fillet, skinned
and cut in chunks

225 g (8 oz) frozen seafood
(e.g., prawns, mussels
and squid)

1 tablespoon chopped parsley

❶ Heat the oil in a large pan. Add the onion, fresh garlic or crumbled Oxo Garlic, Herb and Spice cube, and the pepper and cook gently for 4–5 minutes until softened.

❷ Stir in the canned tomatoes, Oxo Italian Herb and Spice cubes and wine, and then simmer for 10 minutes.

❸ Add the cod and seafood and cook gently for 5–8 minutes more, or until the cod begins to flake. Scatter the parsley over and serve.

Serves 4

Preparation and cooking time:
20–23 minutes

Calories per serving 230

OXO Tip

Try using other varieties of white fish. If using frozen fillets, thaw before cutting up in chunks.

mediterranean grilled
sardines Frozen sardines are
available all year round. They are ideal for
cooking on a barbecue. Serve with salad.

2 Oxo Italian Herb and
Spice cubes

2 tablespoons sunflower oil

12–16 sardines, de-scaled
and cleaned

1 Preheat the grill.
2 Crumble the Oxo Italian
Herb and Spice cubes into
the oil. Brush over the fish
and place them under a hot
grill. Cook for 4–5 minutes,
turn the sardines over,
brush them again and cook
for 4–5 minutes more.
The sardines should be
golden and crispy.

Serves 4

Preparation and cooking time:
10 minutes

Calories per serving 540–730

Tips
Try using other Oxo Herb and
Spice cubes such as Indian.

Sardines are a very good
source of fish oils which are
beneficial to our health.

shallow-fried fillets of plaice Really fresh fish is best for this dish. Serve with new potatoes, a green vegetable and tartare sauce.

4 medium-size plaice fillets,
skinned (page 69)

For the coating
2 Oxo Italian Herb and
Spice cubes
2 tablespoons plain flour
1 large egg
2 tablespoons milk
1 lemon
150 g (5 oz) fresh white
breadcrumbs
oil for frying

❶ Crumble the Oxo Italian Herb and Spice cubes on to a plate. Mix in the flour.
❷ Beat the egg and milk together on a second plate.
❸ Grate the zest from the lemon and mix with the breadcrumbs on a third plate.
❹ Roll each plaice fillet in seasoned flour, dip into the egg mixture and then coat with breadcrumbs.
❺ Pour enough oil into a frying pan to reach a depth of 5 mm ($^1/_4$ inch). Heat until a small piece of bread sizzles on contact.
❻ Turn the heat down slightly and cook the fish, one fillet at a time, for about 2–3 minutes on each side, or until golden.
❼ Lift out and drain on kitchen paper. Keep warm while you cook the remaining fish.

Serves 4
Preparation and cooking time:
30 minutes
Calories per serving 350

OXO **Tip**
Lemon sole fillets would also work well for this dish.

chinese steamed trout
This is a lovely quick dish with lots of Oriental flavour.

a bunch of spring onions
2 tablespoons soy sauce
2 Oxo Chinese Herb and Spice cubes
4 trout, skinned and filleted
175 g (6 oz) Chinese leaves
3 medium-size carrots
1 tablespoon sesame or sunflower oil
1 tablespoon sesame seeds, toasted

1 Finely chop 6 spring onions. Put them in a bowl and add the soy sauce. Crumble in the Oxo Chinese Herb and Spice cubes.
2 Lay the trout fillets, skinned-side up on a board. Spread the spring onion mixture over the fish and then roll them up.
3 Cut the Chinese leaves in shreds. Make carrot shavings using a potato peeler. Cut the remaining spring onions in thin slices.
4 Place the fish in a steamer over a pan of boiling water. Brush them with a little of the oil, and then cover and steam for 6–8 minutes.
5 Heat the remaining oil in a frying pan or wok. Stir-fry the vegetables for 2 minutes. Serve the trout rolls on a bed of stir-fried vegetables and sprinkle with the toasted sesame seeds.

Serves 4
Preparation and cooking time: 15 minutes
Calories per serving 240

Tips
You could ask your fishmonger to fillet and skin the fish, or prepare it yourself (pages 68–69).

If you don't have a steamer you can use a plate placed over a pan of boiling water and then covered with a well-fitting lid.

Toasting the sesame seeds is not essential but it does bring out their lovely nutty flavour. Dry-fry the seeds in a frying pan over a moderate heat. Shake them around the pan and don't take your eyes off them – they will burn in an instant!

Microwave Tip
Place the prepared trout in a microwave dish, cover and cook for 4–5 minutes on HIGH (100%).

poached salmon with creamy tomato sauce

This is an elegant summer dish for when both salmon and good flavoured tomatoes are plentiful. Serve with new potatoes and a green vegetable.

1 carrot, chopped roughly

1 celery stick, chopped roughly

1 Vegetable Oxo cube

4 salmon steaks

sprigs of parsley, to garnish

For the sauce

25 g (1 oz) butter

50 g (2 oz) onion, chopped

450 g (1 lb) ripe tomatoes, skinned, deseeded and chopped roughly

1/2 teaspoon sugar

1 Oxo Italian Herb and Spice cube

4 tablespoons dry white wine

2 tablespoons thick single cream

❶ Melt the butter in a pan, add the onion and cook for 2–3 minutes until soft. Add the tomatoes and sugar. Crumble in the Oxo Italian Herb and Spice cube and add the wine. Simmer uncovered for 15 minutes until pulpy. Sieve, return to the pan and stir in the cream.

❷ Meanwhile, pour 600 ml (1 pint) water into a large frying pan. Add the carrot and celery. Crumble in the Vegetable Oxo cube and bring to the boil. Carefully lower the salmon steaks into the pan, cover and allow to simmer very gently for 6–8 minutes, depending on their thickness.

❸ Lift the salmon out and drain. Garnish with parsley and serve with the sauce.

Serves 4

Preparation and cooking time: 25 minutes

Calories per serving 330

Tip

The sauce can be made ahead and re-heated just before serving.

roast cod with parsley crust This is a simple yet delicious way to serve any flaky fish such as salmon or haddock.

50 g (3 oz) butter
25 g (1 oz) onion, chopped finely
75 g (3 oz) fresh white breadcrumbs
1 Oxo Italian Herb and Spice cube
3 tablespoons chopped parsley
4 x 175–225 g (6–8 oz) cod fillets, skinned (page 69)

1 Preheat the oven to 190°C/375°F/Gas Mark 5. Grease an ovenproof dish with a little of the butter.

2 Melt the remaining butter in a pan, add the onion and cook for 2–3 minutes until softened.
3 Stir in the breadcrumbs and fry until they are lightly golden. Remove from the heat and crumble in the Oxo Italian Herb and Spice cube. Add the parsley.
4 Place the cod fillets in the dish in a single layer. Cover each fillet with the parsley mixture.
5 Cook for 15–20 minutes until firm and opaque.

Serves 4
Preparation time: 15 minutes + 20 minutes cooking
Calories per serving 300

Tips
Make sure that your ovenproof dish is large enough to hold all the fish fillets in a single layer.

Use kitchen tweezers to make sure all the bones have been removed before you add the parsley topping.

crispy fried fish Home-made fish and chips is a real treat, and not too difficult to make. Use any fillets of white fish such as haddock, cod or whiting. Serve with chips.

4 haddock fillets, about 175 g (6 oz) each, skinned

For the batter
1 Vegetable Oxo cube
100 g (4 oz) plain flour
a pinch of salt
1 egg
90 ml (3 fl oz) milk
groundnut or corn oil, for frying

❶ Crumble the Vegetable Oxo cube into 50 ml (2 fl oz) boiling water. Stir well, and then allow to cool. Sift the flour and salt into a bowl and make a well in the centre. Break in the egg and add the stock, beating well with a wooden spoon. Add the milk and beat until smooth.

❷ Fill a deep frying pan or fryer one-third full. Heat until a cube of bread sizzles when dropped in it and browns in 60 seconds.

❸ Dip the fish in the batter, one fillet at a time. Using tongs, lower each fillet separately into the hot oil. Increase the temperature of the oil (adding the fish will lower the temperature).

❹ Cook for 6–8 minutes, turning over halfway, until golden and crisp. You may need to cook the fish in two batches. Lift out and drain on kitchen paper.

Serves 4
Preparation and cooking time: 20–25 minutes
Calories per serving 350

Tip
Before you start check that your haddock fillets aren't too long for your pan. If so, cut them in half.

vegetables

all you need to know:

choosing & storing vegetables

vegetables and a healthy diet

Vegetables play a tremendously important role in our diet. They provide a wealth of vitamins and minerals that are essential for health, growth and vitality. Nutritionists agree that the single most important thing we can do to protect our health is to eat lots of fresh fruit and vegetables.

It was not long ago that we were limited to a small selection of seasonal produce, but now there are all sorts of exotic vegetables from around the world to make our meals more interesting. Moreover, with greenhouse cultivation, local seasons have been extended, and improved methods of farming and transport guarantee consistent quality.

Far from being simply an adjunct to meat, some vegetables, such as onions, garlic and tomatoes, are essential to impart richness and depth of flavour to many recipes. Moreover, many vegetables are substantial enough to be made into delicious vegetarian meals in their own right.

buying vegetables

The turnover of vegetables in supermarkets is so quick that a high level of freshness is usually guaranteed. As you choose your own produce, you can buy exactly the amount you need, as well as picking out the best available. Markets and greengrocers may not be able to compete with the supermarkets in offering such a wide choice of exotic vegetables, but they will often have seasonal and local produce at competitive prices.

The general rule when choosing vegetables is the fresher the better. Buy produce in peak condition

and use it as soon as possible. Root vegetables have a longer life than leaf or green vegetables, so buy more perishable and delicate items, such as salad leaves frequently and in small quantities.

Look for bright, fresh colours and shy away from any leaf vegetable which is limp or beginning to turn yellow. Avoid vegetables that look bruised or soft. Some vegetables deteriorate very quickly, especially in hot weather, so only buy what you can use immediately.

storing vegetables

Root vegetables will keep best in cool, well ventilated conditions. A garage or utility room is preferable to a warm kitchen. Do not store root vegetables in plastic bags as they tend to sweat, and the moisture encourages sprouting and mould-formation. Potatoes turn green when they are stored in the light and develop toxins under the skin. Always cut off any green parts from potatoes before cooking.

Store green and soft vegetables on the lower shelves or in the crisper compartment of the refrigerator. Do not wash vegetables until just before you use them as the water will encourage decay, and vitamins and minerals will be lost.

Store vegetables away from fruit – the smells can transfer and some fruit emit gases that hasten deterioration of vegetables.

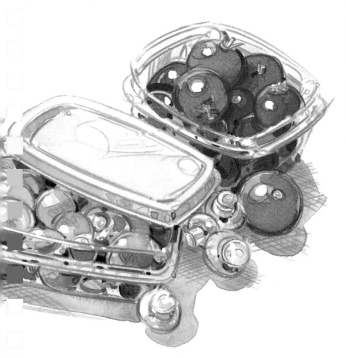

all you need to know:
preparing & cooking vegetables

preparing vegetables

Vegetables require a lot of care in preparation. Trim vegetables sparingly, using a vegetable peeler to remove only the top layer of skin (swivel-bladed peelers are the best). Slice or chop vegetables using a sharp knife, to avoid bruising. Do not soak prepared vegetables in water as this causes vitamins and minerals to leach out. Do not leave prepared vegetables exposed to air and light – cook them as soon after preparation as possible.

dice: casserole recipes often call for diced vegetables. Peel the vegetable and square off the sides. Slice the vegetable vertically, cutting thickly for large dice and thinly for small dice. Cut each piece into uniform strips. Gather the strips into a pile and slice them across to produce evenly-sized cubes.

julienne: these matchstick-sized strips are often used in stir-fries, as they cook very quickly. Cut the peeled vegetable into 5 cm (2-inch) lengths. Then cut each lengthways in thin, vertical slices. Stack the slices and cut them lengthways again into matchsticks.

cooking vegetables

To conserve nutrients and retain flavour, most vegetables benefit from being cooked in only just enough water to cover them. Place root vegetables into cold water, bring to the boil, cover and cook. Plunge leafy vegetables into boiling water and cook briefly.

Steaming takes a little longer than boiling, but is a good alternative, as vegetables retain a higher percentage of nutrients (particularly vitamin C) and often keep a better colour and flavour. Sautéing and stir-frying are also good cooking methods as they are quick, allowing the vegetables to keep their colour and texture.

Baking and braising are equally effective, as few nutrients are lost. Braising is done in a small amount of liquid, such as water, stock or wine, with a little oil or butter. This tasty cooking liquid can then be eaten with the vegetables. Vegetables are delicious when roasted. Root vegetables, tomatoes, peppers, aubergines, courgettes, whole garlic cloves and mushrooms can all be roasted. Starchy root vegetables need to be peeled and parboiled beforehand. Drain them well and let them air-dry in the hot pan. For a really crisp texture, roughen the surface with a fork. Toss into hot oil and roast for 1 hour, until the vegetables are well browned and crisp. It may help to increase the oven temperature to 220°C/ 450°F/Gas Mark 8 to finish them off – you can do this while the joint is resting before carving. More delicate vegetables can be cut in halves or chunks as appropriate, brushed with oil and roasted for 30–45 minutes.

Microwaving is a fast and healthy way to cook vegetables, as very little water is needed and cooking times are relatively short.

all you need to know:
a – z of seasonal vegetables

asparagus (May–July)
Wash and cut off the woody part of the stem. Tie in bundles and cook upright in a deep saucepan, so that the tougher stems cook in the water and the delicate tips are steamed. Cover the tips with foil and simmer gently for 8–12 minutes.

aubergine (available all year round) Choose firm, shiny aubergines. Halve or slice them and sprinkle generously with salt; leave for 30 minutes to drain off any bitter juices. Rinse and pat dry with kitchen paper.

broad beans (April–July)
Choose young, tender pods. Allow 225 g (8 oz) of whole pods per person. Remove the beans from the pods and cook them in boiling salted water for 8–10 minutes.

beans, french (available all year round) Choose crisp pods with smooth skins. Trim the ends and boil or steam for 8–10 minutes.

runner beans (July–October)
Choose beans that break with a crisp snap. Trim the ends, remove any strings and cut into slices or chunks. Boil or steam for 10 minutes.

broccoli/calabrese (available all year round) Choose firm, tightly packed heads. Trim the stalks and leaves and halve the florets, if large. Simmer for 7–10 minutes, or steam for 10 minutes.

cabbage, green (available all year round) Choose fresh looking cabbage with no wilted leaves. Cut in half, remove the centre stalk and shred the leaves. Cook in boiling water or steam for 3–5 minutes. Allow 175–225 g (6–8 oz) per person.

cabbage, red or white (available all year round)
Slice or shred and use raw in salads. Shred and casserole red cabbage with spices and a little sugar and red-wine vinegar. Cover and cook for about an hour at a low/medium heat.

carrots (available all year round) Choose firm, bright orange carrots with smooth skins. Trim the ends, peel thinly and then slice, dice, or cut in batons. Eat raw with dips, or boil in salted water for 10–15 minutes or steam for 12–18 minutes.

cauliflower (available all year round) Choose firm, white heads with fresh green leaves. Cauliflower is usually removed from its stalk and divided into florets. Cook in boiling water or steam for 5–7 minutes.

celeriac (September–March) Choose heads which are firm and heavy. Peel thickly and cut into slices or julienne strips. Cook in boiling, salted water for 20 minutes, or blanch strips to use in salads.

celery (available all year round) Look for tightly closed stalks with fresh, green leaves. Separate the stalks, scrub them and trim the ends. Use raw in salads or cut into thick slices and braise.

courgettes (available all year round, best in summer) Choose small to medium-size firm courgettes, with smooth, shiny, dark green skins. Trim the ends, wash and slice, dice or cut in batons. Cook in boiling salted water, steam or sauté in butter for 5 minutes.

leeks (available all year round) Choose leeks with firm bulbs still attached to their roots, and bright green tops. Trim the roots and top. Slice lengthways, spread open to expose the layers and rinse well under running water to remove any grit. Cook in boiling, salted water for 8–10 minutes, steam for 10–12 minutes or braise and serve with butter and salt.

mangetout (available all year round) These are an under-developed pea and you eat the whole pod. Cook in boiling water for 2 minutes or halve and use them in stir-fries.

mushrooms (available all year round) Choose fresh looking mushrooms, with smooth-skinned caps. Wipe with a damp cloth and trim the end of the stalk. Sauté in a little butter or oil.

onions (available all year round) Choose firm onions, with tight, shiny skins. Spanish onions are larger, have a mild flavour and can be eaten raw in salads. Red onions have a mild, sweet flavour and can also be eaten raw.

To chop an onion, peel the onion and halve it lengthways through the root end. Holding the onion by the root end, cut off the shoot end and discard. Slice the onion vertically, the knife tip towards the root. Keep the root intact as this will hold the slices in place as you cut. Now slice at right angles to the vertical cuts and then discard the root and chop to size if necessary.

parsnips (August–April) Choose small to medium-size parsnips, with firm, unblemished skins. Trim both ends and peel thinly. Slice or cut in chunks. Boil or steam for 10–15 minutes or parboil for 2 minutes and then roast them around a joint of meat.

peas (June–October) Choose plump, crisp pods. Allow 225 g (8 oz) peas in the pod per person. Shell the peas, rinse and cook in boiling, salted water for 5 minutes.

peppers (available all year round) Peppers should be firm, with a smooth skin and bright colour. To deseed, cut a slice off the top, using a sharp knife, and then remove the core and seeds under running water.

potatoes (available all year round) Choose firm potatoes with smooth unbruised skin without cracks or sprouting eyes. Buy new potatoes in small quantities and use them up quickly.

Prepare potatoes just before cooking to retain as much vitamin C as possible. Scrub or scrape new potatoes and boil them in salted water for 15 minutes, until tender.

Peel and quarter main-crop potatoes and boil them for 15–20 minutes to make them into mashed or creamed potatoes. Cut them into chips and deep-fry them, or bake large potatoes in their jackets. Peel, quarter and parboil potatoes before roasting them in oil or dripping, either on their own or around a joint. To sauté potatoes, boil them for 10 minutes, drain well and cut them in large chunks. Shallow-fry in hot oil and butter until crisp and golden.

spinach (available all year round) Look for bright, fresh, undamaged leaves that are neither broken, limp nor wilted. Spinach shrinks a lot when cooked, so allow 175–225 g (6–8 oz) raw spinach per person.

Remove the stalks and wash spinach thoroughly in a sinkful of water. Cover and cook without any added water for 4–5 minutes, until the leaves have wilted. Drain well using a sieve.

swede (available all year round) Choose small swede, with firm flesh and smooth skin. Peel thickly, cut in chunks and boil or steam for 20 minutes.

sweetcorn (home-grown July–October; imported all year round) Choose cobs with a pale green, closely fitting husk – the kernels should look plump and juicy. Remove the husks and silky fibres and cook in boiling, unsalted water for 10–15 minutes.

tomatoes (available all year round) There are many varieties to choose from – always look for firm, unblemished skins. To skin, cut a small slit in the skin, place in a bowl and pour boiling water over. Leave for about 30 seconds, or until the skin wrinkles and bursts open. Drain and slip the skins off.

turnips (small early turnips April–July; main-crop available all year round) Choose turnips that are smooth and unblemished, with crisp green tops, if attached. Peel young turnips thinly and cook them whole. Peel older ones thickly, and slice or cut them in chunks. Boil in salted water for 15–20 minutes, until tender.

baked stuffed aubergines

This dish is based on a Turkish recipe and is equally delicious hot or cold. Serve with a salad and rustic-style bread.

2 large aubergines or 4 small aubergines

4 tablespoons olive oil

2 large onions, chopped

2 Oxo Garlic, Herb and Spice cubes

450 g (1 lb) ripe tomatoes, skinned and chopped (page 89)

1 tablespoon tomato purée

1/2 teaspoon ground cinnamon

25 g (1 oz) raisins

1 tablespoon lemon juice

25 g (1 oz) pine kernels (optional)

3 tablespoons chopped parsley

salt and pepper

❶ Cut the aubergines in half lengthways. Score the flesh with a sharp knife, sprinkle with salt and set aside for 1/2 hour to draw out the bitter juices.

❷ Preheat the oven to 180°C/350°F/Gas Mark 4.

❸ Rinse the aubergines under cold running water and pat dry with kitchen paper. Using a small knife, scoop out the flesh (taking care not to damage the skin) until you have a shell about 5 mm (1/4 inch) thick. Chop the flesh.

❹ Heat half of the oil in a large frying pan, add the onions and fry for 5 minutes until soft and lightly coloured.

❺ Add the rest of the oil. Stir in the chopped aubergine and fry for 5 minutes, stirring constantly.

❻ Crumble in the Oxo Garlic, Herb and Spice cubes. Add the tomatoes, tomato purée, cinnamon, raisins, lemon juice and pine kernels (if using). Season with salt and pepper. Allow to cook gently for 5 minutes and stir in the parsley.

❼ Place the aubergine shells close together in an ovenproof dish and spoon in the stuffing. Cover with foil and bake for 1–1 1/4 hours until the aubergine shells are cooked and the flesh looks translucent. Serve hot or cold.

Serves 4

Preparation time: 25 minutes + 1 1/2 hours cooking

Calories per serving 230

☉☓☉ Tips

Plum tomatoes would be excellent in this recipe because they have more flavour.

Choose similar sized and shaped aubergines to ensure even cooking.

≋ Microwave Tip

Put the onions and half of the oil in a large microwave dish. Cover and cook on HIGH (100%) for 3–4 minutes. Add the chopped aubergine and cook for 5 minutes. Stir in the rest of the ingredients and cook for 5 minutes longer. Arrange the aubergine shells on a platter, brush them with the remaining oil and cook on HIGH (100%) for 7–8 minutes, or until tender. Fill the shells with the stuffing and re-heat for 2 minutes.

broccoli and tuna gratin
This is very quick and easy to prepare. The fresh taste of the broccoli complements the creamy cheese sauce.

450 g (1 lb) broccoli florets

400 g (14 oz) canned tuna
in brine, drained

For the cheese sauce

40 g (1½ oz) butter

3 tablespoons flour

600 ml (1 pint) milk

1 Oxo Italian Herb and
Spice cube

175 g (6 oz) Red Leicester
cheese, grated

50 g (2 oz) fresh breadcrumbs

salt and pepper

1 Put the broccoli in a pan of boiling water and cook for 5 minutes until just tender. Drain.

2 For the sauce, melt the butter in a large pan, add the flour and cook for 1 minute. Gradually stir in the milk. Crumble in the Oxo Italian Herb and Spice cube and bring to a simmer, whisking constantly.

3 Remove from the heat and stir in two-thirds of the cheese. Season if necessary.

4 Stir the tuna and broccoli into the sauce and heat for 1–2 minutes. Spoon into an ovenproof dish.

5 Preheat the grill. Mix the breadcrumbs with the remaining cheese and scatter over the top of the dish. Place under the grill and cook until golden brown.

Serves 4

Preparation and cooking time:
20–25 minutes

Calories per serving 510

Tips

You can easily turn this into a dish for vegetarians by leaving out the tuna. Cook 175 g (6 oz) pasta, drain and add to the broccoli and sauce.

This dish can be prepared in advance and refrigerated. Re-heat in a moderate oven for 20 minutes.

Microwave Tip

Place the broccoli florets in a large bowl with 4 tablespoons of water. Cover and cook on HIGH (100%) for 6–7 minutes, stirring once. To make the sauce, melt the butter for 45 seconds on HIGH (100%) and stir in the flour. Add the milk, crumble in the seasoning cube and cook for 3–5 minutes more, stirring twice, until the sauce thickens. Continue with recipe from step 4.

mushroom bruschetta This
makes a lovely starter or light lunch.

4 thick slices Italian bread or 8 thick slices baguette

3 tablespoons olive oil

1 Oxo Garlic, Herb and Spice cube

25 g (1 oz) butter

4 spring onions, chopped

450 g (1 lb) mushrooms, sliced

4 tablespoons thick Greek-style yogurt

1 tablespoon chopped parsley

salt and pepper

1 Preheat the oven to 200°C/400°F/Gas Mark 6.

2 Brush both sides of the bread with the oil and place on a baking sheet. Crumble half of the Oxo Garlic, Herb and Spice cube over the slices. Bake for 10 minutes until crisp.

3 Heat the butter in a frying pan. Sauté the spring onions for 1 minute, and then add the mushrooms and the remaining half of the seasoning cube.

4 Cook over a high heat until the mushrooms are golden. Stir in the yogurt and season with salt and pepper. Spoon on to the garlic bread and scatter over the chopped parsley.

Serves 4

Preparation and cooking time: 15 minutes

Calories per serving 290

Tips

Try out some of the different types of mushrooms now available, such as chestnut or oyster. For a special treat include some fresh wild mushrooms.

Pugliese bread is ideal for bruschetta – you may well find some in your local supermarket. Ciabatta will also work.

celery and apple soup Soups are not difficult to make, and with just a few ingredients they can provide a very economical dish for the family. Serve with crusty bread and tasty cheese.

1 head celery

25 g (1 oz) butter

1 small onion, chopped

2 Vegetable Oxo cubes

450 g (1 lb) Bramley apples, peeled, cored and chopped

150 ml (1/4 pint) single cream

salt and pepper

❶ Remove the celery leaves and set aside. Chop the stalks.
❷ Melt the butter in a large saucepan. Add the chopped celery and onion and stir. Cover the pan and cook over a low heat for 10 minutes.

❸ Meanwhile, crumble the Vegetable Oxo cubes into 900 ml (1 1/2 pints) boiling water.
❹ Add the apples and stock to the pan. Simmer for 15–20 minutes.
❺ Purée the soup in a blender or food processor until smooth. Return to the pan, stir in the cream and season if necessary.
❻ Garnish with the celery leaves.

Serves 4

Preparation and cooking time: 35 minutes

Calories per serving 180

(OXO) **Tip**
Try grating some nutmeg on top of the soup before serving. This will add a pretty garnish and a hint of extra flavour.

❄ **Freezing Tip**
Most soups freeze beautifully. Add any cream, yogurt or garnishes to soups when reheating.

spinach filo pie 'Filo' is the Greek word for leaf. Filo pastry is wafer-thin and leaf-like so it doesn't need rolling out and is ready to use from the packet.

450 g (1 lb) frozen leaf
spinach, thawed

6 spring onions, chopped

225 g (8 oz) cottage cheese

4 tablespoons chopped parsley

2 Vegetable Oxo cubes

3 eggs

40 g (1½ oz) butter, melted

225 g (8 oz) filo pastry, thawed
if frozen

❶ Preheat the oven to 180°C/350°F/Gas Mark 4.

❷ Press as much excess water from the spinach as possible. Place it in a large bowl and add the spring onions, cottage cheese and parsley.

❸ Crumble in the Vegetable Oxo cubes. Beat the eggs and mix well with the other ingredients.

❹ Lightly brush a 23 cm (9-inch) loose-bottomed cake tin or deep flan tin with some of the butter. Brush a sheet of filo pastry with more butter and place it in the tin. Repeat, using about two-thirds of the sheets to line the tin. They should overlap each other and hang over the edge of the dish. Make sure there are no gaps in the pastry lining.

❺ Spoon in the spinach filling. Fold the edges of the pastry over the filling. Place the remaining pastry sheets on top of the pie, cutting them to fit if necessary. Tuck the corners in between the tin and pie. If you prefer, you can scrunch up the remaining sheets and lay them on top.

❻ Brush the top of the pie with butter and bake for 25–30 minutes until crisp and golden.

Serves 4

Preparation time: 15 minutes
+ 30 minutes cooking

Calories per serving 360

OXO Tip

Keep filo pastry covered with a damp cloth to prevent it drying out while you prepare the pie.

curried potato salad This is a dream of a dish for potato lovers – new potatoes in a creamy sauce with just a hint of spice.

700 g (1½ lb) baby new
potatoes

1 tablespoon oil

1 medium-size onion,
chopped finely

2 Oxo Indian Herb and
Spice cubes

150 ml (¼ pint) soured cream
or crème fraîche

2 tablespoons mayonnaise

1 tablespoon lemon juice

2 tablespoons chopped fresh
coriander or parsley

1 Cook the potatoes in lightly salted boiling water for about 20 minutes until tender. Drain and allow to cool.

2 Heat the oil in a frying pan. Cook the onion until soft and lightly browned.
3 Crumble in the Oxo Indian Herb and Spice cubes. Cook over a low heat for 2 minutes and then turn into a bowl to cool.
4 Add the soured cream or crème fraîche, mayonnaise and lemon juice to the onions. Mix everything together. Halve the potatoes and gently fold them in. Garnish with coriander or parsley.

Serves 4

Preparation and cooking time:
25 minutes

Calories per serving 290

Tips

If you like sweet flavours in your curried dishes, try adding a handful of raisins.

Waxy old potatoes can be used instead of new potatoes – but don't let them overcook.

boston baked beans Canned
beans save cooking time. This recipe is child's play and very economical. Serve with crusty bread.

1 tablespoon sunflower oil

1 large onion, chopped

4 rashers rindless smoked back bacon, cut in 1 cm (1/2-inch) pieces

397 g can of chopped tomatoes

2 tablespoons tomato purée

1 Original Oxo cube

2 tablespoons dark brown sugar

2 teaspoons prepared English mustard

a pinch of dried chilli flakes (optional)

425 g can of red kidney beans, drained

425 g can of cannellini or haricot beans, drained

1 tablespoon chopped parsley

1 Heat the oil in a large flameproof casserole. Add the onion and bacon and fry for 4–5 minutes until golden.

2 Stir in the tomatoes and tomato purée. Crumble the Original Oxo cube into 300 ml (1/2 pint) boiling water. Stir into the pan with the sugar, mustard and chilli flakes (if using).

3 Add the beans to the pot. Cover and simmer gently for 45 minutes. Stir in the parsley and serve.

Serves 4–6

Preparation time: 10 minutes + 45 minutes cooking

Calories per serving 330

Tip

For vegetarians, leave out the bacon and the Original Oxo cube. Substitute 100 g (4 oz) chopped mushrooms and a Vegetable Oxo cube.

❄ Freezing Tip

This recipe freezes beautifully.

lentil and cauliflower curry

Lentils are a good source of protein. Together with the cauliflower they make a nourishing and tasty dish.

1 tablespoon sunflower oil

1 large onion, chopped

2 Oxo Indian Herb and
Spice cubes

1 Vegetable Oxo cube

100 g (4 oz) red lentils

397 g can of chopped
tomatoes

1 medium-size cauliflower,
divided in florets

salt and pepper

1 Heat the oil in a large saucepan and cook the onion for 4–5 minutes until lightly browned. Crumble in the Oxo Indian Herb and Spice cubes. Stir together for 1 minute.

2 Crumble the Vegetable Oxo cube into 300 ml (½ pint) boiling water and add to the pan.

3 Put the lentils in a sieve and wash them under cold running water. Add the rinsed lentils and tomatoes to the pan. Cover and simmer for 15 minutes.

4 Add the cauliflower and cook for 10–15 minutes until the cauliflower is tender. Stir two or three times during cooking and season if necessary.

Serves 4

Preparation and cooking time:
35 minutes

Calories per serving 160

Tip
Lentils can absorb a lot of water. Keep an eye on the saucepan and add a little extra water if the curry seems to be getting too dry.

Microwave Tip
Cook the onion and oil in a large bowl on HIGH (100%) for 2 minutes. Add the Oxo Indian Herb and Spice cubes, vegetable stock, lentils and tomatoes, and cook for 10 minutes, stirring twice. Stir in the cauliflower and cook for 8–10 minutes more.

Freezing Tip
Vegetable curries freeze very successfully. Try to season foods when reheating as salty foods do not freeze very well.

braised vegetables with garlic crumbs This is a truly delicious way to cook root vegetables. Cook them with your Sunday joint.

2 large carrots

3 medium-size parsnips

350 g (12 oz) swede

2 tablespoons olive oil

25 g (1 oz) butter

8 baby onions

8 baby potatoes

1 Vegetable Oxo cube

salt and pepper

For the garlic crumbs

50 g (2 oz) butter

1 Oxo Garlic, Herb and Spice cube

100 g (4 oz) coarse breadcrumbs

1 Preheat the oven to 180°C/350°F/Gas Mark 4.
2 Cut the carrots and parsnips in pieces about 4 cm (1½ inches) long, and then cut each piece into four lengthways. Cut the swede into similar size chunks.
3 Heat the oil and butter in a large shallow flameproof casserole. Add all of the vegetables and cook until lightly browned.
4 Crumble the Vegetable Oxo cube into 240 ml (8 fl oz) boiling water. Pour over the vegetables and season to taste. Cover and braise for 45 minutes, or until the vegetables are tender.
5 For the garlic crumbs, heat the butter in a frying pan, crumble in the Oxo Garlic, Herb and Spice cube and fry the breadcrumbs for about 5 minutes, stirring constantly until golden and crisp.
6 Scatter the crumbs over the top of the vegetables just before serving.

Serves 4

Preparation time: 20 minutes + 55 minutes cooking

Calories per serving 310

Tips

The recipe can be adapted to whichever root vegetables are in season. Try celeriac, kohlrabi or turnips.

The easy way to make breadcrumbs is to use a food processor, if you have one.

If you are serving this as a main course you may like to add 100 g (4 oz) grated cheese to the topping.

Microwave Tip

Brown the vegetables in a frying pan and then transfer them to a large, shallow microwave dish. Add the stock, cover and cook on HIGH (100%) for 18–20 minutes, stirring twice.

Freezing Tip

You can prepare the vegetables in advance (up to the end of step 4) and freeze them. Make the crumbs just before you need them.

rice & pasta
all you need to know:
choosing & storing
rice & pasta

Pasta and rice are cheap, nutritious and truly versatile; easy to prepare, they can be served as accompaniments or used as the main ingredient in a dish. Essential as storecupboard standbys, they are the ultimate convenience foods, always on hand for the busy cook to make into quick and tasty meals.

pasta and rice and a healthy diet

Pasta and rice have become as important as potatoes in the British diet as a staple source of carbohydrate. As we are encouraged to make different carbohydrate foods the focus of our meals, pasta and rice are very important for healthy eating today.

Pasta is a simple food, made from durum wheat, salt and water, sometimes enriched with eggs. High in carbohydrate with hardly any fat, it is a filling and healthy ingredient.

Rice is one of the world's most healthy staples as its complex carbohydrates are digested slowly, allowing the body to use the energy released over a longer period of time. Low in sodium, it contains B vitamins, potassium and virtually no fat. Rice is also gluten-free and easily digested.

choosing pasta

Both fresh and dried pasta are sold in an ever-increasing variety of shapes, colours and flavours. Many shapes were conceived for particular dishes, such as lasagne sheets for layering, or cannelloni tubes for stuffing. Hollow and ridged shapes are designed to hold thick chunky sauces, while long thin pastas such as spaghetti are better suited to more viscous sauces. Oriental noodles, used in Chinese, Japanese and Asian cooking, are most often sold dried.

Fresh pasta is available in many supermarkets and delicatessens, and is the nearest thing to home-made pasta you will find. Made from flour and eggs, fresh pasta needs only the briefest cooking, and will easily end up mushy. Fresh filled pastas include tortellini, ravioli and cannelloni which have a wide range of fillings, such as cheese, spinach, mushroom, meat, ham and even smoked salmon.

Dried pasta is completely different from fresh pasta. Made from durum wheat, salt and water, dried pasta is convenient to have in the cupboard and many people prefer it, as it has more 'bite' than fresh.

Quick-cook pasta can be ready in 3–5 minutes. No-precook lasagne sheets are used straight from the packet and do not need pre-boiling. They tend to absorb a lot of the liquid from the sauce, so the lasagne can end up fairly solid. Read the pack instructions about adding extra liquid.

storing pasta

Fresh pasta will keep in the refrigerator for a few days – use it before the sell-by date on the box, if pre-packed.

For white rice, the husk and bran layers are removed in the milling to produce a white grain. Once cooked, the grain becomes fluffy. Easy-cook rice, sometimes known as parboiled, converted or pre-fluffed rice, is virtually impossible to overcook.

Long-grain brown rice, also known as whole-grain rice, undergoes only partial milling, which removes the husk but leaves the bran layer intact. Brown rice has a nutty flavour and a higher fibre, vitamin and mineral content than white rice. It is also available in easy-cook form, which has a slightly less chewy texture than regular brown rice.

storing rice

Rice will keep for a long time, but look for the best-before date on the packet. Store unopened packets in a cool, dry cupboard. Once opened, transfer to an air-tight container.

Cool leftover rice quickly, cover and refrigerate it for up to 2 days, or freeze it. Do not leave cooked rice at room temperature.

Filled shapes are a useful standby to have in the freezer. Freeze on the day of purchase. They can be cooked from frozen if you allow an extra 2 minutes.

Store dried pasta in a cool, dry cupboard. Opened packets are best emptied into a clean, airtight storage jar, as dried pasta can become brittle and lose its flavour when exposed to air.

choosing rice

There are a large number of rice varieties available. The individual characteristics of each rice will determine its suitability for a particular dish, although many people use all-purpose long-grain rice for everything.

all you need to know:
types of rice & pasta

pasta

fresh pasta: this is the closest to home-made pasta and is particularly worth buying for filled pasta, such as tortellini or ravioli. Shown here are fresh tagliatelle and fresh ravioli.

spaghetti: this pasta comes in long, straight strands of varying thickness, and is available in various colours and in quick-cook and wholemeal varieties.

tagliatelle: flat ribbon-shape pasta very similar to fettuccine and available in plain, spinach and tomato flavours, and sometimes with added herbs or garlic.

conchiglie (shells): range from tiny soup shapes to very large ones, which can be stuffed.

penne (quills): made in various sizes, ribbed or plain.

fusilli (twists): come in different sizes and can be plain or coloured.

macaroni: short-cut or elbow macaroni are small, thin, hollow shapes.

vermicelli: fine-cut pasta, often sold in little nests or clusters.

lasagne: the 'traditional' sort of dried lasagne needs some cooking before the layers are filled, but it is

also available in no-precook varieties. No-precook is very convenient but you may find that traditional gives a moister finished dish.

farfalle: these pretty shapes look like bows, but the Italian name means 'butterflies'.

egg noodles: available in thin or medium-thick sizes.

rice noodles: available in various thicknesses, they require only soaking in hot water for 10–15 minutes before using.

rice

basmati rice: known as the 'Prince of Rice'. A slender long-grain rice, grown in the foothills of the Himalayas, it has a unique fragrance and delicate texture. Easy-cook and brown basmati are also available.

thai fragrant rice (jasmine): another aromatic rice, with a soft and slightly sticky texture once cooked, it is good with Chinese and south-east Asian food.

risotto rice (arborio): medium-grain, Italian rice, risotto absorbs as much as five times its weight in liquid. During cooking, starches are released, to give the creamy texture of the classic risotto.

wild rice: not a true rice, but an aquatic grass, the grains are long, slim and range in colour from dark brown to black. The flavour is very intense and nutty, so it is usually sold mixed with white rice and par-cooked.

vermicelli

tagliatelle

fresh tagliatelle

rice noodles

egg noodles

farfalle

thai fragrant rice

fusilli

risotto rice

basmati rice

wild rice

fresh ravioli

macaroni

conchiglie

tagliatelle

penne

spaghetti

lasagne

all you need to know:
cooking rice & pasta

cooking pasta

Pasta is one of the easiest foods to cook. It helps if you have a very large saucepan that can hold up to 4 litres (7 pints) of water. A large sieve or colander is also useful to have on hand.

easy steps for perfect pasta

Allow between 50 and 100 g (2–4 oz) of pasta per person, depending on whether you are serving it for a starter or as a main course.

Put the pasta into a large saucepan of fast-boiling, salted water. Allow 2–3 litres (3$\frac{1}{2}$–5$\frac{1}{2}$ pints) of water per 450 g (1 lb) pasta. A dash of oil will help to separate the pasta and prevent the strands or shapes from sticking to each other.

● Once it begins to cook, give the pasta a good stir. When cooking spaghetti, add it all to the pan at once and gently push it into the boiling water as it softens.

● Keep the water at a steady boil – lower the heat to prevent it from boiling over.
● The cooking time for dried pasta depends on its size. Follow packet instructions for best results as some cook quicker than others. Fresh pasta usually takes only 2–3 minutes.
● To test if the pasta is cooked, bite a piece. It should be *al dente*, meaning just tender, with a little firmness left. Make sure you don't overcook the pasta – it will become sticky and soggy. Once it is cooked, drain it immediately.
● For pasta that is to be cooked further, as for lasagne, or for a cold pasta salad, leave the pasta slightly undercooked, as it will absorb more moisture as it bakes or cools. Rinse salad pasta in cold water and dress it as soon as possible, to prevent it sticking together.

cooking rice

During cooking, the starch in rice swells, the grain softens and the rice increases in size. Allow 50 g (2 oz) uncooked rice per person as an accompaniment and slightly more if it is to be used as the main course.

Some types of rice should be rinsed before cooking, including basmati, ordinary long-grain, glutinous and wild rice. Place the rice in a bowl, add plenty of cold water and swirl the grains around. Drain off most of the water and repeat several times, until the water stays clear. Drain in a sieve.

easy steps for cooking perfect rice

● **absorption:** in this method, just enough cold liquid is added to the rice, so that by the end of the cooking time the rice is tender and all the liqiud has been absorbed. Use the table to measure the correct quantities of rice, water and salt into a saucepan. Bring to the boil, stir once and lower the heat until just simmering.

● **open-pan:** this is the easiest method for many cooks. Pour the rice into a large pan of boiling, salted water and cook until tender. Drain off excess liquid using a sieve or colander. It's helpful to

Cooking times for rice

| Types of rice | quantity | | cooking times (minutes) | |
	rice (g)	liquid (ml)	hob	oven (180°C/ 350°F/ Gas Mark 4)
long-grain	250	500	12–15	40
long-grain easy-cook	250	550	18	45
basmati	250	450	10	35
basmati easy-cook	250	600	12	40
long-grain brown	250	625	35	1 hour 15
long-grain brown easy-cook	250	650	30	1 hour 10
basmati brown	250	600	25	50
jasmine	250	450	10	35
wild	250	750	45	1 hour 40
medium-grain (risotto)	250	1 litre	30	-
convenience rices		check packet instructions		

All timings are an average approximation. Check packet instructions.

leave the rice to drain over the pan for a few minutes, stirring it very gently.

● **microwave:** this is a convenient method of cooking rice, as it can be cooked and served in the same dish. However, because it needs to stand for 10 minutes after cooking, microwaved rice takes just as long to cook as other methods. During the standing time it will continue to cook and absorb liquid. Do not cook more than 350 g (12 oz) at a time, as it tends to bubble up during cooking.

● **oven-baking:** this is a slow method of cooking rice, but useful if you're cooking a casserole in the oven at the same time.

Use the quantities of rice and water given for the absorption method and place them in an ovenproof dish with a well-fitting lid.

● To test if rice is cooked, remove a few grains with a fork and press one between thumb and finger – if it separates cleanly with no hard core, it is ready.
● Leftover rice can be kept for up to two days in the refrigerator. Reheat it in a saucepan with some oil or a few tablespoons of water, or cover and reheat it in the oven.

spring green vegetable risotto
Risottos should be cooked and served straight away.

2 Vegetable Oxo cubes

100 g (4 oz) fine green beans, cut in 2.5 cm (1-inch) lengths

2 tablespoons olive oil

225 g (8 oz) courgettes, halved lengthways and sliced

25 g (1 oz) butter

6 spring onions, chopped

350 g (12 oz) Italian risotto rice

150 ml (1/4 pint) dry white wine

100 g (4 oz) frozen peas

25 g (1 oz) parmesan cheese, freshly grated + extra to serve

1 Crumble the Vegetable Oxo cubes into 900 ml (1½ pints) boiling water.

2 Bring a small pan of water to the boil. Add the beans and cook for 2 minutes. Drain.

3 Heat the oil in a deep frying pan with a lid. Add the courgettes and cook for 2–3 minutes. Lift out with a slotted spoon.

4 Add the butter to the pan. Stir in the spring onions and cook for 1 minute. Add the rice and cook over a medium heat, stirring constantly, until transparent.

5 Add the wine and bring to a boil. Pour in half of the stock. Cover the pan and simmer for about 10 minutes until the liquid has been absorbed.

6 Stir in the rest of the stock and cook for 5 minutes. Add all the vegetables and cook for about 5 minutes more, or until the rice is tender and the mixture has a creamy consistency. Remove from the heat and stir in the parmesan cheese. Sprinkle with a little extra parmesan cheese and serve.

Serves 4

Preparation and cooking time: 30 minutes

Calories per serving 470

Tips

You will get the creamiest risotto if you use Italian risotto rice.

If the risotto soaks up all of the liquid before the rice is cooked and tender, stir in a little extra water.

Microwave Tip

Prepare the beans and courgettes as per the recipe. Melt the butter in a large microwave dish, add the spring onions and rice and cook on HIGH (100%) for 3 minutes. Add the wine and half the stock, cover and cook for 10 minutes. Stir in the remaining stock and cook for 10 minutes more. Add the vegetables, cover and cook for 2–3 minutes. Allow to stand for 5 minutes and then stir in the parmesan.

pasta with roasted
vegetables If you haven't yet
tried roasted vegetables you'll find their lovely sweet, rich flavours almost addictive.

4 medium-size courgettes, cut in 5 mm (¼-inch) thick slices

2 small red onions, cut in 6 wedges

2 red peppers, deseeded and cut in thick slices

4 tomatoes, quartered

3 tablespoons olive oil

350 g (12 oz) dried tagliatelle

For the sauce

2 Oxo Garlic, Herb and Spice cubes

50 g (2 oz) walnuts

2 tablespoons chopped parsley

5 tablespoons olive oil

1 Preheat the oven to 220°C/425°F/Gas Mark 7.

2 Place all the vegetables in a roasting tin. Drizzle with the olive oil and roast for 25 minutes or until tender.

3 Meanwhile, cook the pasta in a large pan of lightly salted boiling water until *al dente*. Drain and return to the pan.

4 Put the Oxo Garlic, Herb and Spice cubes, walnuts, parsley and oil in a food processor. Blend together until the nuts are finely chopped.

5 Add the sauce and vegetables to the pasta and toss everything together.

Serves 4

Preparation and cooking time: 30 minutes

Calories per serving 870

Tip
Vegetables cooked in this way are also delicious when eaten cold, either on their own or mixed with cooked pasta to make a pasta salad. If you don't want to use the walnut sauce, try sprinkling the vegetables with the crushed seasoning cube before roasting.

creamy pasta twists
This pasta dish can be put together in minutes. Serve with a mixed green salad.

350 g (12 oz) pasta twists	
25 g (1 oz) butter	
175 g (6 oz) diced ham	
225 g (8 oz) Brie cheese	
1 Oxo Garlic, Herb and Spice cube	
240 ml (8 fl oz) single cream	
black pepper	

Serves 4

Preparation and cooking time:
15 minutes

Calories per serving 680

(OXO) **Tip**

You can substitute 225 g (8 oz) sliced mushrooms for the ham.

❶ Cook the pasta in a large pan of lightly salted boiling water for 8–10 minutes until *al dente*. Drain.

❷ Meanwhile, melt the butter in a frying pan. Add the ham and cook for 2–3 minutes.

❸ Remove the rind from the cheese. Chop it roughly and add to the pan. Crumble in the Oxo Garlic, Herb and Spice cube and stir in the cream.

❹ Heat gently until the cheese has melted.

❺ Add the pasta, season with black pepper, toss together and serve.

pasta soup Pasta makes simple soups tastier and more filling.

2 tablespoons olive oil

1 medium-size onion, chopped

2 celery sticks, chopped finely

2 Chicken Oxo cubes

450 g (1 lb) ripe tomatoes, skinned and chopped

1 Oxo Garlic, Herb and Spice cube

50 g (2 oz) small pasta shapes

salt and pepper

chopped parsley, to garnish

1 Heat the oil in a large saucepan. Add the onion and celery and cook gently until softened.

2 Crumble the Chicken Oxo cubes into 1.1 litres (2 pints) boiling water. Pour into the pan and add the tomatoes and Oxo Garlic, Herb and Spice cube.

3 Bring to a simmer and cook for 2 minutes. Add the pasta. Cook, uncovered, for 10–12 minutes until the pasta is tender. Season if necessary, and garnish with chopped parsley before serving.

Serves 4–6

Preparation and cooking time: 25 minutes

Calories per serving 145

Tip

To make this soup even more substantial you could add a can of borlotti or haricot beans.

Freezing Tip

This soup will freeze successfully for up to 3 months.

spicy rice supper For the best flavour the rice should be cooked well ahead so that it has time to cool off. It can then be stir-fried with the other ingredients just before serving.

250 g (9 oz) long-grain rice
1 Chicken Oxo cube
2 tablespoons groundnut or vegetable oil
3 shallots or 1 medium-size onion, chopped
1/2 teaspoon chilli powder
1 teaspoon paprika
1 large carrot, grated coarsely
225 g (8 oz) piece of cooked ham, cut in small chunks
100 g (4 oz) peeled prawns, thawed if frozen
50 g (2 oz) frozen peas, thawed
salt and pepper

1 Put the rice in a sieve and rinse well under cold running water.
2 Bring 600 ml (1 pint) of water to the boil in a saucepan, crumble in the Chicken Oxo cube and stir. Add the rice, cover and simmer for 12 minutes, or until the stock is absorbed and the rice is just tender. Set aside to cool.
3 Heat the oil in a large frying pan, add the shallots or onion and cook for 4–5 minutes until soft and lightly brown.
4 Stir the spices into the shallots or onion. Add the carrot and ham and cook for 3 minutes.
5 Add the cooled rice, breaking it up with a wooden spoon. Add the prawns and peas and stir-fry for 3–4 minutes until heated through. Season if needed.

Serves 4
Preparation and cooking time: 25 minutes + 2 hours cooling
Calories per serving 380

Tips
Substitute cooked chicken for the ham, and add other vegetables such as shredded cabbage for a change.
Once the rice is cool it should be refrigerated if you're not using it right away.

Microwave Tip
To cook the rice in the microwave, place the rice and boiling stock in a large bowl and cook on HIGH (100%) for 5 minutes. Reduce the power to MEDIUM (50%) and cook for 10–15 minutes more, or until the liquid is absorbed and the rice is tender.

roast stuffed peppers

Different coloured peppers would look really pretty in this dish. Serve with a crisp green salad and crusty bread.

50 g (2 oz) long-grain rice

2 tablespoons olive oil

1 medium-size onion, chopped

2 Oxo Italian Herb and Spice cubes

432 g can of borlotti beans or chick-peas, drained

150 g (5 oz) mozzarella cheese, chopped in small pieces

4 medium-size red peppers

salt and pepper

❶ Cook the rice in lightly salted boiling water for about 10 minutes until only just tender. Drain.

❷ Preheat the oven to 200°C/400°F/Gas Mark 6.

❸ Heat half the oil in a frying pan. Cook the onion for about 4–5 minutes until soft and golden. Crumble in the Oxo Italian Herb and Spice cubes. Cook for 1 minute and then turn into a bowl.

❹ Add the rice, beans or chick-peas and cheese. Season with salt and pepper.

❺ Cut the tops off the peppers and discard the core and seeds, reserving the lids. Divide the filling between the peppers, packing it in firmly.

❻ Replace the lids, drizzle with the remaining oil and bake for 30 minutes, until the peppers are tender and are slightly charred around the edges.

Serves 4

Preparation time: 15 minutes + 30 minutes cooking

Calories per serving 310

(OXO) **Tip**

If the peppers are wobbly, slice a thin strip off their undersides so that they balance upright.

smoked haddock kedgeree
This makes an excellent light meal and a wonderful weekend brunch. Use undyed smoked haddock (page 66).

350 g (12 oz) smoked haddock fillet

175 g (6 oz) long-grain rice

25 g (1 oz) butter

1 small onion, chopped finely

1 Oxo Indian Herb and Spice cube

100 g (4 oz) peeled prawns, thawed and drained if frozen

1 tablespoon lemon juice

2 eggs, hard-boiled and chopped

2 tablespoons single cream

2 tablespoons chopped parsley

salt and pepper

1 Put the haddock in a frying pan. Add 300 ml (½ pint) water. Bring to a simmer and poach gently for 8–10 minutes. Lift out the fish and drain the liquid from the pan. Flake the haddock with a fork, discarding the skin and any visible bones.

2 Cook the rice in boiling salted water for 12–15 minutes. Drain, rinse and then drain again.

3 Melt the butter in the frying pan. Add the onion and cook for 3–4 minutes until softened.

4 Crumble in the Oxo Indian Herb and Spice cube. Stir for 1 minute and add the rice, haddock, prawns and lemon juice.

5 Add the eggs, cream and parsley. Season if necessary.

Serves 4

Preparation and cooking time: 35 minutes

Calories per serving 350

OXO Tip

Drain the rice well or you will end up with a soggy kedgeree. You could also try this dish with canned pink salmon: drain the fish, remove the skin and bones and break it up slightly before adding to the pan.

oriental pasta salad with peanut sauce This is a delicious light lunch.

100 g (4 oz) medium Chinese noodles
1/2 cucumber, cut in small pieces
1/2 bunch of spring onions, chopped
1 red pepper, deseeded and cut in thin strips
2 tablespoons salted peanuts, chopped roughly

For the peanut sauce
2 Oxo Chinese Herb and Spice cubes
2 tablespoons crunchy peanut butter
2 tablespoons sunflower oil

1 Cook the noodles as directed on the packet. Drain, rinse under cold water and drain again. Put into a bowl and allow to cool. Take care not to overcook the noodles. If they are too soft they will become unpleasantly mushy when added to the salad

2 To make the sauce, crumble the Oxo Chinese Herb and Spice cubes into a small bowl. Add 3 tablespoons boiling water and stir until the cubes have dissolved. Add the peanut butter and oil and whisk until well blended. Allow to cool.

3 Add the vegetables and sauce to the noodles. Mix together and transfer to a serving dish. Scatter with the peanuts.

Serves 3–4
Preparation and cooking time: 15–20 minutes
Calories per serving 350

(OXO) **Tip**
If the sauce is too stiff to fold easily into the noodles, simply whisk in a little extra hot water.

spaghetti bolognaise Don't be put off by the number of ingredients: this recipe is really very simple. All the different flavours blend together to make a rich, tasty sauce.

2 tablespoons olive oil

2 rashers streaky bacon, chopped (optional)

1 small onion, chopped

1 celery stick, diced (optional)

1 small carrot, diced

1 garlic clove, crushed or

1 Oxo Garlic, Herb and Spice cube

350 g (12 oz) lean minced beef

1 Original Oxo cube

397 g can of chopped tomatoes

2 tablespoons tomato purée

1 Oxo Italian Herb and Spice cube

salt and pepper

For the pasta

350 g (12 oz) spaghetti

1 tablespoon olive oil

freshly grated parmesan cheese, to serve

1 Heat the oil in a large pan. Add the bacon, if using, and cook for 2 minutes. Add the onion and cook for 3 minutes, or until beginning to soften. Stir in the celery, carrot and fresh garlic (if using). Cook for 2 minutes and then crumble in the Oxo Garlic, Herb and Spice cube (if using).

2 Stir in the mince and cook until it changes colour, breaking up any lumps with a wooden spoon.

3 Crumble the Original Oxo cube into 150 ml (¼ pint) boiling water. Pour into the pan. Add the tomatoes and tomato purée. Crumble in the Oxo Italian Herb and Spice cube. Stir well and bring to a simmer. Cover and cook over a low heat for 45 minutes, stirring occasionally. Season with salt and pepper if necessary.

4 15 minutes before the sauce is cooked, bring a large pan of lightly salted water to the boil. Add the spaghetti and cook for 10 minutes or until *al dente*.

5 Drain the pasta. Return it to the pan and toss with the olive oil. Serve with the bolognaise sauce and parmesan cheese.

Serves 4

Preparation time: 15 minutes + 1 hour cooking

Calories per serving 660

⊙⌾⊙ **Tips**

If you find the sauce is getting too thick, simply add a little water. You could add 3 or 4 finely chopped sun-dried tomatoes, if you have any. They will give an extra richness to the sauce.

Other types of pasta such as tagliatelle or fettuccine will work equally well.

≋ **Microwave Tip**

Place the oil, bacon, onion, celery, carrot and crushed garlic or Oxo Garlic, Herb and Spice cube in a large bowl with the minced meat. Cook on HIGH (100%) for 5 minutes, stirring once. Add the remaining sauce ingredients and cook for 8 minutes more, stirring twice. Lower the temperature setting to MEDIUM (50%) for 10 minutes longer.

❄ **Freezing Tip**

This sauce freezes beautifully for up to 3 months.

classic lasagne Few dishes have proved quite so popular in recent years as really scrumptious melting lasagne. This is the classic recipe.

1 quantity of bolognaise sauce (page 123)

225 g (8 oz) lasagne

2 tablespoons grated parmesan cheese

For the sauce

600 ml (1 pint) semi-skimmed milk

1 bay leaf

50 g (2 oz) butter

50 g (2 oz) plain flour

100 g (4 oz) Cheddar cheese, grated

salt and pepper

❶ Heat the milk with the bay leaf in a saucepan until it is not quite at boiling point. Remove from the heat and stand for 10 minutes. Discard the bay leaf.

❷ Meanwhile, melt the butter in a heavy saucepan. Sprinkle in the flour and cook for 1 minute over a gentle heat, stirring constantly.

❸ Remove the pan from the heat and gradually stir in the milk. Return the pan to the heat, stir until thick and smooth, and season with salt and pepper.

❹ Bring a large pan of salted water to the boil. Cook the sheets of lasagne in two batches until just tender. They will need about 10 minutes each. Drain thoroughly and spread out on a clean tea towel.

❺ Preheat the oven to 180°C/350°F/Gas Mark 4. Grease a rectangular 1.7-litre (3-pint) ovenproof dish.

❻ Arrange a layer of lasagne sheets over the base of the dish. Spoon over half the bolognaise sauce. Drizzle with 5 tablespoons of the sauce.

❼ Repeat the layers, finishing with a layer of lasagne sheets.

❽ Add the Cheddar cheese to the remaining sauce. Spread over the top, covering the surface completely. Sprinkle with the parmesan cheese.

❾ Bake for 45 minutes, or until the top is golden.

Serves 4

Preparation time: 30 minutes + 45 minutes cooking

Calories per serving 830

Tips

This dish may be prepared in advance and either stored in the fridge for a couple of hours before baking, or frozen.

Try using lasagne verde (spinach-flavoured lasagne) for a change.

No-precook lasagne does save time but the traditional variety gives a moister, more tender result.

Microwave Tip

Cook the assembled lasagne for 25–35 minutes on MEDIUM (50%), rotating the dish halfway through. Allow the lasagne to stand for 15 minutes before serving.

Freezing Tip

Freeze at the end of step 8. If you don't want your lasagne dish to be out of commission for weeks in the freezer, try the following: once the lasagne is frozen, remove from the freezer and run hot water over the base of the dish to loosen the frozen block of lasagne. Place the lasagne in a freezer bag and label it. When you want to cook the lasagne, place it back into the original dish and thaw thoroughly before baking.

eggs & cheese

all you need to know:
choosing & storing eggs & cheese

eggs and a healthy diet

Eggs provide many of the nutrients essential for a healthy balanced diet and are one of the most complete and nutritious foods available. They contain a wide range of minerals, including iron and calcium, and are rich in vitamin B12 and vitamin D. Although low in fibre and carbohydrate, they are high in protein, and a size-3, or medium, egg has only 80 calories. Eggs do contain cholesterol and this has made people wary about eating them, but it is recognised that the amount of saturated fat you eat will have more effect on the health of your heart than the amount of cholesterol you consume. Research has shown that most people on a low-fat diet can eat up to seven eggs a week, without increasing their blood cholesterol levels.

cheese and a healthy diet

Cheese is one of the most nourishing foods, containing as much protein and calcium weight for weight as many other main body-building foods. Cheese is also useful in cooking as it adds flavour and bulk. Cheese can be made from goats' or ewes' milk as well as cows' milk; both give a distinctive flavour.

choosing eggs

Always buy from a reputable source, either a supermarket with a quick turnover, or a registered local producer. Under EC regulations, there are three grades of eggs, A, B and C. Class A are the highest grade and are usually the only ones available in the shops. The colour of the eggs does not indicate quality, but only the particular breed of hen. Both brown and white shelled eggs have the same nutritional value.

Look for the Lion Mark on egg cartons – this symbol represents the new standards for eggs sold in Britain, which are higher than those required by EC law. Egg cartons specify how the hens have been kept while laying.

Battery eggs: these are often labelled 'Farm Fresh' or 'Country' eggs. 85% of eggs produced in the UK are battery-raised.

Barn or perchery eggs: these are from hens that are reared in barn-like buildings. The hens move freely in the building, lay in nesting boxes and have natural light, but no outdoor access.

Free-range eggs: these are from hens that roam freely and live on wheat, maize and farmyard scraps. These eggs may have a better flavour than battery eggs but are no more nutritious. All cartons should also indicate size, a 'best-before' date and the egg producer's name and code.

Eggs range in size from the largest, size 0 (about 75 g/3 oz), down to size 5 (about 50 g/2 oz). Generally, smaller eggs than these are not sold in supermarkets, but small or pullet eggs can sometimes be bought from farms. Size 3 is the medium egg size and should be used in these recipes, unless otherwise stated. Remember to check the 'best-before' date, to make sure you have at least seven days to use the eggs.

storing eggs

Store eggs in the refrigerator, in their cartons with the narrow ends downward, to reduce evaporation. Eggs should be kept away from strong-smelling foods, as their shells are porous and may absorb odours.

Keep eggs away from uncooked foods, as they easily spoil through cross-contamination. As with all perishable foods, eggs should be handled hygienically. Wash your hands before and after handling them and discard any cracked eggs.

Eggs are best used at room temperature – take them out of the refrigerator about 30 minutes before cooking.

choosing cheese

Always buy from a reputable supplier or supermarket. Cheese should be kept chilled or cool, depending on the variety. When buying pre-packed cheese, make sure it does not look sweaty, and check the 'use-by' date. If the date is many weeks ahead, the cheese may be immature.

Many supermarkets have introduced a number system to indicate how strong or mild a cheese tastes, or the label may simply specify mild, medium or mature. Whatever your preference, choose cheese that looks fresh and even in texture and colour.

storing cheese

Store cheese in the bottom of the refrigerator or in a dairy box. Wrap each piece in greaseproof paper and then in foil, or place in an airtight container. Allow the cheese to come to room temperature while still in its wrapper if it is to be served with crackers or bread. Cheese used in cooking should be kept refrigerated until it is used.

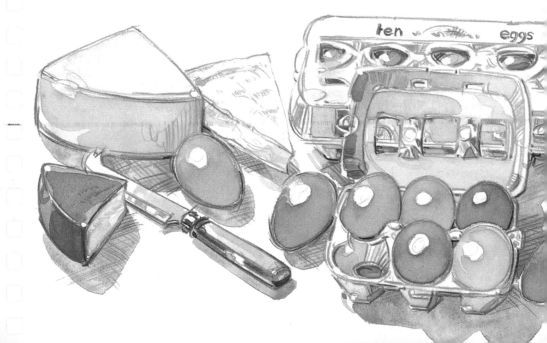

all you need to know:
types of cheese

english medium cheddar

Cheese is a solid derivative of milk. After the curds are separated from the whey the solids form cheese which is then ripened. During the ripening or maturing process, its taste, texture and appearance changes, and each variety of cheese will take on a particular flavour.

Semi-hard cheeses include Cheddar and Edam, which tend to be used in everyday cooking. Cheddar can vary in flavour from very mild to fully matured and strong. Hard cheeses are long matured, with a low moisture content, but may still contain up to 50 per cent fat. They include parmesan and pecorino, and because they have a strong flavour and can be finely grated, a little goes a long way.

Lower-fat hard cheeses are produced from semi-skimmed milk and can help to reduce one's fat intake. Lower-fat Cheddar contains about half as much fat and approximately two-thirds of the calories of traditional Cheddar.

Vegetarian cheese is available in a few varieties such as Cheddar, double Gloucester, Stilton and Mozzarella. These cheeses are made using vegetarian rennet.

Soft cheeses such as Brie and Camembert are generally eaten with biscuits or bread, but can also be used in cooking. They are ripened briefly and contain a high percentage of moisture and fat.

Fresh cheese is unripened curd, eaten shortly after it is made. Many fresh cheeses have low-fat alternatives, all of which can be used in cooking. Examples include fromage frais (a good substitute for cream), cottage cheese, curd cheese and cream cheese.

mild white cheddar

gruyère

mature blue stilton

dolcelatte

vegetarian red leicester

double gloucester

traditional farmhouse cheddar

red leicester

cheshire

edam

mozzarella

feta

half-fat red leicester

pecorino romano

camembert

half-fat cheddar

blue stilton

brie

parmesan

mature camembert

all you need to know:
cooking eggs & cheese

cooking eggs

The Department of Health currently recommends avoiding eating raw eggs or uncooked foods made with them. For healthy people, there is very little risk from eating eggs which are lightly cooked. More vulnerable are those people such as the elderly, the sick, babies and toddlers and pregnant women, who are advised to consume only eggs which have been cooked until the whites and yolks are solid.

Egg dishes should be eaten as soon as possible after cooking, or stored in the fridge and reheated thoroughly before consuming.

easy steps to perfect eggs

● **boiled:** bring the eggs to room temperature and then gently lower them into a saucepan of simmering water. Alternatively, cover the eggs with cold water and bring them to the boil. The cooking should be timed from when the water begins to boil. Hard-boiled eggs should be drained, cracked and rinsed under running water to cool them as quickly as

possible. This prevents a black ring from forming around the yolk as the egg cools.

soft-boiled eggs

size 1-3	3 minutes
size 4-7	2 minutes

firm white, soft yolk

size 1-3	4 minutes
size 4-7	3 minutes

hard-boiled eggs

size 1-3	10 minutes
size 4-7	8 minutes

● **poached eggs:** these work best using really fresh eggs. Fill a frying-pan with water 4 cm (1-inch) deep, bring the water to a simmering point and add 2 teaspoons of vinegar. Crack the egg into a small bowl and then slide it into the water (see picture below).

Keep the heat low and poach for 2–3 minutes. Do not allow the water to boil as the egg will

toughen. Baste the egg carefully with water (see picture below).

Remove from the frying-pan with a slotted spoon. Eggs can be poached in stock or wine to give extra flavour.

● **fried eggs:** heat a little oil in a frying-pan over a moderate heat. Break one egg at a time into the pan and baste the edges of the eggs with the fat as they

cook (see picture above). Cook until the white is just set and firm, and then remove the egg from the pan using a fish slice.

● **scrambled eggs:** beat the required number of eggs with a little seasoning. Melt a knob of butter in a non-stick saucepan over a moderate heat. Add the eggs and cook over a gentle heat, stirring all the time, paying particular attention to the sides and bottom of the pan (see picture below).

Scrambled eggs are cooked when they are firm, but creamy (see picture below). Remove from the heat and serve at once.

● **baked eggs:** preheat the oven to 180°C/350°F/Gas Mark 4. Grease an ovenproof ramekin dish and break an egg into it. Season with salt and pepper and then dot with flecks of butter. Spoon a teaspoon of single cream over the egg and bake for about 10 minutes, or until the white is set but the yolk still soft.

● **omelettes:** to make an omelette, beat 2 eggs with a tablespoon of cold water and season with salt and pepper. Heat a little olive oil or a knob of butter in an omelette pan with curved sides. When the fat is hot, add the beaten eggs. Using a palette knife or spatula, draw the mixture from the sides into the middle of the pan, allowing the uncooked egg to run into the base of the pan and set (see picture below).

When the base is firm and pale golden, the top should still be soft like scrambled egg (see picture below).

Add your filling (if desired) and fold over to serve.

cooking with cheese
Some cheeses become stringy when heated, which is fine when making a fondue or topping pizzas, but not so good when you're aiming for a smooth sauce. Gruyère and Jarlsberg are good strong, 'chewy' cheeses for fondues, while mozzarella is many peoples' favourite pizza topping. Mature Cheddar will give a good flavour to a sauce – always heat cheese slowly when adding it to a sauce as a fierce heat will make it stringy. Firm but crumbly cheeses such as feta, Stilton and Cheshire will give the best texture to salads.

ricotta and leek pancakes
Pancakes can be kept in the freezer, ready to be filled for quick family meals.

100 g (4 oz) plain flour

a pinch of salt

2 eggs

300 ml (¹/₂ pint) milk

butter for frying

For the filling

40 g (1¹/₂ oz) butter

225 g (8 oz) leeks, chopped finely

2 Oxo Garlic, Herb and Spice cubes

225 g (8 oz) ricotta cheese

3 tablespoons sesame seeds

❶ Put the flour, salt, eggs and milk in a blender or food processor and blend until smooth. (Or you could follow the instructions on page 138 for preparing batter.)

❷ Melt a small knob of butter in a 20.5 cm (8-inch) heavy-based frying pan. Pour in about 2 tablespoons of batter, or enough to thinly coat the base of the pan. Cook the pancake over a medium heat until set. Lift the side with a palette knife to check that it is golden brown. Turn the pancake and cook the other side until golden.

❸ Repeat until all the batter is used up, adding butter to the pan as needed.

❹ Preheat the oven to 180°C/350°F/Gas Mark 4.

❺ For the filling, melt two-thirds of the butter in a frying pan. Add the leeks and cook gently for 5 minutes until softened.

❻ Crumble in the Oxo Garlic, Herb and Spice cubes and mix well. Turn into a bowl and stir in the cheese.

❼ Place a tablespoon of the filling at one end of each pancake. Fold the sides over and then roll them up. Place the filled pancakes in an ovenproof dish.

❽ Melt the remaining butter and brush over the filled pancakes. Scatter with the sesame seeds and bake for 20 minutes until golden.

Serves 4

Preparation and cooking time: 45 minutes

Calories per serving 460

Tip

The bolognaise sauce on page 123 would make an excellent filling for these pancakes. Scatter with some grated parmesan or Cheddar cheese before baking.

Microwave Tip

You can cook the assembled pancakes in the microwave on HIGH (100%) for 8 minutes.

Freezing Tip

You can prepare these pancakes up to the end of step 7 and freeze them for up to 3 months. Thaw well before baking.

fail-safe cheese soufflé

Soufflés are not expensive or difficult to make, and they're a real delight to eat.

50 g (2 oz) butter

50 g (2 oz) plain flour

2 Oxo Italian Herb and
Spice cubes

300 ml (½ pint) milk, warmed

100 g (4 oz) mature Cheddar
cheese, grated

4 eggs, separated

❶ Use 15 g (¼ oz) of the butter to grease a 1.4-litre (2½-pint) soufflé dish – make sure the inside of the rim is well coated. Dust the inside with a teaspoon of the flour.

❷ Preheat the oven to 200°C/400°F/Gas Mark 6.

❸ Melt the remaining butter in a large heavy-based saucepan. Blend in the flour and stir over a low heat for 1 minute. Crumble in the Oxo Italian Herb and Spice cubes. Remove from the heat and gradually blend in the milk.

❹ Cook over a medium heat, stirring constantly, until the sauce becomes very thick and smooth. Remove from the heat and beat in the egg yolks, one at a time. Stir in the cheese until melted.

❺ Whisk the egg whites in a large grease-free bowl until stiff. Add a third of the egg whites to the sauce. When these have combined thoroughly, carefully fold in the rest with a large metal spoon.

❻ Turn into the prepared dish and place on a baking tray in the oven. Turn the heat down to 190°C/375°F/Gas Mark 5 and cook for 25–30 minutes until the soufflé is well puffed up and golden brown. Serve immediately.

Serves 4

Preparation time: 10 minutes
+ 30 minutes cooking

Calories per serving 370

Tips

A straight-sided dish is essential so that the soufflé rises evenly. The baking tray will make the soufflé easier to handle and also helps it cook evenly.

25 minutes cooking time will give a soufflé which is just a little runny in the centre and 30 minutes will ensure that it is firm throughout.

potato skins with dolcelatte dip
Potato skins are a great favourite with children. This is a wonderful starter for anyone who loves blue cheese.

4 medium-size baking potatoes

3 tablespoons olive oil

1 Oxo Italian Herb and Spice cube

100 ml (4 fl oz) milk

100 g (4 oz) Dolcelatte cheese, rind removed and chopped in small pieces

4 tablespoons crème fraîche

2 teaspoons cornflour

1 Place the potatoes in a pan of lightly salted water. Bring to the boil and cook for 15 minutes. Drain and allow to cool.

2 Preheat the oven to 200°C/400°F/Gas Mark 6.

3 Cut the potatoes in quarters and scoop out most of the flesh, leaving a shell 5 mm (¼-inch) thick.

4 Brush the outside of the skins with olive oil. Place on a baking sheet. Then brush the insides with olive oil and crumble the Oxo Italian Herb and Spice cube over the potatoes. Bake for 30 minutes until crisp and golden.

5 Put the milk and cheese in a saucepan and heat gently, stirring until smooth.

6 Blend the crème fraîche with the cornflour. Add to the pan and cook for 3 minutes, whisking all the time until thick and creamy. Serve alongside the potato skins.

Serves 4

Preparation time: 20 minutes + 30 minutes cooking

Calories per serving 270

Tips

If your family find the taste of Dolcelatte too strong, use a milder-flavoured creamy cheese.

Save the potato flesh to use as a topping for a cottage pie or other oven bake. Alternatively, mash it and serve it up with some tasty sausages.

greek island quiche

For the pastry

- 175 g (6 oz) plain white flour
- 40 g (1½ oz) hard margarine
- 40 g (1½ oz) white vegetable fat
- 3–4 tablespoons cold water
- salt

For the filling

- ½ bunch of spring onions, chopped
- 1 red pepper, deseeded and chopped
- 100 g (4 oz) feta cheese
- 15 g (½ oz) butter
- 100 g (4 oz) courgette, cubed
- 2 Oxo Garlic, Herb and Spice cubes
- 2 eggs
- 100 ml (4 fl oz) milk
- 50 ml (2 fl oz) single cream

1. Sift the flour with a pinch of salt. Add the margarine and fat and rub together with your fingertips until the mixture resembles fine breadcrumbs. Add 3–4 tablespoons cold water and mix together until the mixture clings together to make a dough.
2. Form into a ball. Knead lightly on a floured surface until smooth. Roll out to fit a 23 cm (9 inch) quiche or flan tin.
3. Lift the pastry on to the rolling pin and place it over the tin. Gently ease the pastry into the tin, pressing lightly into the corners. Do not try to stretch it upwards to fit as it will shrink during cooking. Chill for 30 minutes.
4. Preheat the oven to 200°C/400°F/Gas Mark 6.
5. Put the spring onions and pepper in a bowl. Crumble in the cheese.
6. Heat the butter in a frying pan. Add the courgette and fry for 2–3 minutes until slightly softened. Crumble in the Oxo Garlic, Herb and Spice cubes. Mix together and add to the bowl.
7. Line the chilled pastry case with foil. Place on a baking sheet and bake for 10 minutes. Remove the foil and cook for 5 minutes until set and pale golden. Remove from the oven and reduce the temperature to 180°C/350°F/Gas Mark 4.
8. Spoon the onion and cheese filling into the flan case. Beat the eggs, milk and cream together. Pour over the filling. Bake for 35–40 minutes, or until the filling is set. Serve warm or cold.

Serves 4

Preparation time: 20 minutes + 30 minutes chilling + 40 minutes cooking

Calories per serving 475

OXO Tip

For any flan, tart or quiche it's a good idea to part-bake the pastry case before adding the filling. This ensures nice crispy pastry.

herby mince popovers
Popovers are small, individual-size versions of toad-in-the-hole. They can contain a variety of tasty fillings.

For the batter

100 g (4 oz) plain flour

2 eggs

300 ml (¹/₂ pint) semi-skimmed milk

salt

For the filling

1 small onion, grated

350 g (12 oz) lean minced beef

2 tablespoons chopped parsley

¹/₂ teaspoon mixed dried herbs

¹/₄ teaspoon grated nutmeg

1 Original Oxo cube

8 teaspoons sunflower oil

salt and pepper

❶ Sift the flour with a pinch of salt into a bowl. Make a well in the centre and break in the eggs. Add a little milk and beat in the flour. Add the remaining milk and beat well until slightly frothy.
❷ Preheat the oven to 220°C/425°F/Gas Mark 7.
❸ Put the grated onion, minced beef, parsley and dried herbs and nutmeg in a bowl.
❹ Crumble the Original Oxo cube into 1 tablespoon hot water. Stir and add to the mince.

❺ Mix well. Divide into 4 rough mounds.
❻ Take 4 gratin dishes about 13–15 cm (5–6 inches) in diameter. Add 2 teaspoons of oil to each. Heat in the oven for 5 minutes.
❼ Place a portion of the filling in the middle of each dish and pour some batter around it.
❽ Bake for 10 minutes, and then reduce the temperature to 200°C/400°F/Gas Mark 6 for 20 minutes, or until puffy and golden brown.

Serves 4

Preparation time: 25 minutes + 30 minutes cooking

Calories per serving 380

Tips
The dishes will be easier to take in and out of the oven if you place them all on a baking sheet.

The batter can be made in advance and kept in the fridge until needed.

caramelised onion and cheese parcels Serve these
tasty pies with a mixed green salad.

25 g (1 oz) butter
450 g (1 lb) onions, sliced
3 tablespoons thick Greek-style yogurt or crème fraîche
2 Oxo Italian Herb and Spice cubes
350 g (12 oz) puff pastry
100 g (4 oz) Gruyère or Gouda cheese, cut in thin strips
1 egg yolk, beaten

❶ Melt the butter in a heavy frying pan. Cook the onions over a low heat, stirring often, for about 30 minutes. The onions will turn a brown-caramel colour.

❷ Mix together the yogurt or crème fraîche and Oxo Italian Herb and Spice cubes.

❸ Roll the pastry out until it measures about 25 cm (10 inches) square. Cut it in four smaller squares.

❹ Imagine a line going from one corner of each square to the diagonally opposite corner. On one side of this line spread a quarter of the onions. Top with a spoonful of the yogurt and add some cheese.

❺ Dampen the edges of the square and fold in half along your imaginary line to make a triangular parcel. Press the edges together, trimming if necessary.

❻ Tap the pastry edges together with the blunt edge of a knife. This helps to seal the edges. Brush the parcels with the beaten egg yolk. Place on a baking tray and chill for 15 minutes. Heat the oven to 200°C/ 400°F/Gas Mark 6.

❼ Bake the parcels for 15 minutes or until puffy and golden.

Serves 4

Preparation and cooking time:
45 minutes

Calories per serving 660

Tips

Ready-rolled frozen puff pastry is ideal for this dish and will save some time.

These are best eaten right away while puffy and hot.

bacon and leek bake This makes a lovely supper on a chilly day. Serve with warm crusty bread.

700 g (1½ lb) small potatoes, peeled

1 tablespoon olive oil

225 g (8 oz) thick rashers rindless bacon, cut in thick strips

1 large onion, sliced

8 oz (225 g) Bramley apples, peeled, cored and diced

2 medium-size leeks, sliced thickly

1 Vegetable Oxo cube

4 tablespoons fresh breadcrumbs

For the cheese sauce

25 g (1 oz) butter

25 g (1 oz) plain flour

300 ml (½ pint) semi-skimmed milk

1 teaspoon prepared English mustard

100 g (4 oz) mature Cheddar cheese, grated

salt and pepper

❶ Put the potatoes in a pan of lightly salted water. Bring to the boil, cook for 10 minutes, and then drain.

❷ Heat the oil in a large frying pan. Add the bacon and fry for 4–5 minutes until golden brown. Remove from the pan.

❸ Add the onion to the pan and cook over a medium heat for 10 minutes until soft and golden, stirring to prevent it burning.

❹ Add the apple and leeks. Cook for 5 minutes. Crumble the Vegetable Oxo cube into 6 tablespoons hot water. Add to the pan and simmer for 2 minutes. Stir in the bacon, and then transfer to a large shallow ovenproof dish.

❺ Cut the cooked potatoes into 5 mm (¼-inch) slices. Arrange them on top of the bacon mixture, overlapping the slices.

❻ Preheat the oven to 190°C/375°F/Gas Mark 5.

❼ Put the butter, flour and milk into a saucepan. Cook over a gentle heat, stirring constantly until smooth and thickened. Stir in the mustard and three-quarters of the cheese. Season if necessary.

❽ Pour the sauce over the potatoes and top with the breadcrumbs and remaining cheese. Bake for 20–25 minutes until golden and bubbling.

Serves 4

Preparation and cooking time: 1 hour

Calories per serving 650

Tip

A whisk is a great help when making sauces. Be sure to stir the cheese sauce constantly to keep it smooth.

Microwave Tip

Microwave the assembled dish on HIGH (100%) for 10 minutes.